To Seth,

grandfather[?]

friend Aurel, who will [?]

day be a famous member of

our society.

Yours, Henk Pelson

HENK'S WAR

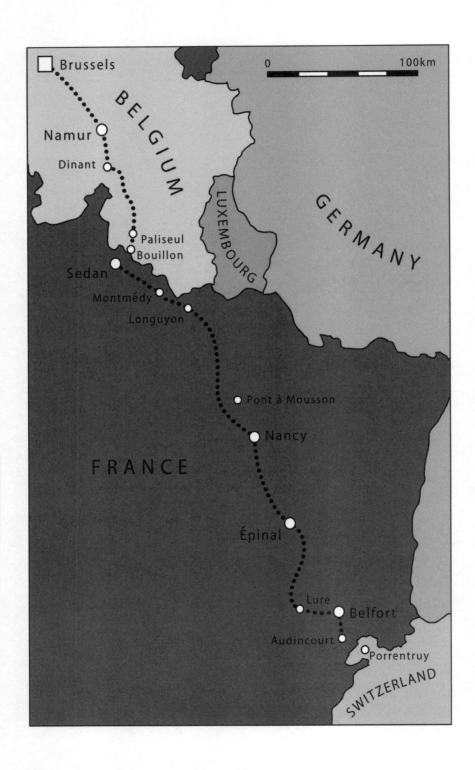

HENK'S WAR

BY HENK E. PELSER, M.D., PH.D.

PP

Portell Production

London

Original title:

Vluchtweg Zwitserland, Verhalen uit een ondergronds verleden

published 1996; Uitgeverij Bert Bakker, Amsterdam

ISBN 90 351 1787 5

Published by

Portell Production

35 Fournier Street

London

E1 6QE

+44 (0)20 7375 1563

portell@dial.pipex.com

ISBN 0-9552720-0-9

ISBN 978-0-9552720-0-4

Designed by Roland Codd

Produced by Robert Paulley

Printed in The United Kingdom by Biddles Ltd, King's Lynn

DEDICATION

For Dries and for my grandschildren Wardit, Martha,
Fedde, Alexander and Sebastian

"A WORD OF THANKS"

I want to remember first of all my travel companions Dries Ekker and
Mathieu Smedts who both contributed so much to the substance of this
book but sadly never saw it published. I want to thank my dear friends
Mau Frenkel and Ward Messer who so generously allowed me to make
use of their memoirs to complement my own. I am most grateful to
Hans Warendorf jr. who encouraged, criticised and did so much to
make publication of both the Dutch and the English versions possible. I
wish to thank Stichting Democratie en Media for their moral and
financial support. I owe a big hug and a thank you to Robert Paulley
who, having patiently listened to my stories since childhood, convinced
me to write them down and who now, together with his wife Linda
Duffin, has put so much energy and professionalism into publication of
the English version. And last but not least I want to thank my elder
daughter Simcha von Benckendorff who not only contributed her
considerable linguistic and language skills but who has also
unremittingly bullied, cajoled and encouraged and made sure this book
came to be.

INTRODUCTION

LIFE IN HOLLAND DURING THE OCCUPATION

At daybreak on Friday May 10th 1940, Hitler's *Wehrmacht* crossed the Dutch border without any formal declaration of war. The German attack came as a severe shock to the Dutch who were essentially unprepared for war since they had been confident that their neutrality would be respected as it had been during the First World War.

Within a few hours the *Luftwaffe* had virtually wiped out the Dutch air force before it could even get airborne and German paratroopers had penetrated into the very heart of *Fortress Holland*, the fortified centre of the country. It was decided that Crown Princess Juliana together with her husband, the German-born Prince Bernhard, and their two small daughters should be taken to safety and, on the evening of Sunday May 12th, they were smuggled to the port of IJmuiden to board the British destroyer HMS *Codrington* and taken across the Channel.

The very next morning, Queen Wilhelmina was advised by General Winkelman, the Dutch Commander-in-Chief, that the military situation was deteriorating alarmingly. She decided that she too should leave the country. Accompanied by just a few aides the Queen was escorted to Hook of Holland from whence the destroyer HMS *Hereward* took her to Harwich.

Prodded into action by the Queen's decisiveness, the Dutch Cabinet now agreed not to capitulate to the Nazis, but rather to set aside constitutional objections, go into exile and continue to govern the Dutch overseas colonies from Britain, where it had been offered sanctuary. A decree was issued vesting the Commander-in-Chief of the Dutch Army with all powers necessary to govern the European territory of the Kingdom of the Netherlands. The Cabinet then boarded the British destroyer HMS *Windsor* and left for England only a few hours after the departure of their Queen.

The German Supreme Command had badly underestimated the resistance that the Dutch army would put up and they soon got worried that their *Blitzkrieg* strategy might be endangered by the unexpected delay. Hitler and Goering therefore decided to launch an air raid on Rotterdam. On 14 May the *Luftwaffe* devastated the centre of Rotterdam and when the Nazis threatened the same treatment to other Dutch cities, General Winkelman capitulated. The German occupation of the Netherlands had begun.

CURFEWS AND QUISLINGS

Much to the relief of the Dutch, the Germans seemed to govern with a light hand. There were, of course, almost inevitable inconveniences. A curfew was imposed after midnight but black-outs made being outside after dark a dodgy business anyway. The Dutch electronics manufacturer Philips brought a "dyno torch" on the market - a contraption powered by a dynamo which was worked by rhythmically squeezing and releasing a handle on the body of the torch. As a source of light it was rather haphazard and, as the sound it produced resembled nothing so much as the howling of a tortured cat, it was soon universally known as a *knijpkat* (literally, a "squeeze-cat").

The one single measure to be taken by the Nazis that would have the most pervasive effect on Dutch society was the reorganisation of the police. Prior to the German occupation, the Dutch police was rather decentralised and consisted of five distinct forces which ultimately reported to one or more of the Ministries of Defence, Justice or Home Affairs. The first of these obviously ceased to exist with the advent of the occupation. Throughout the period of occupation, it would remain the general policy of the Dutch caretaker administration to regard any form of resistance to the German authorities as useless and even detrimental to the Dutch national interest. In line with this policy, it was decided to strengthen the police force and tighten its grip on the population in order to be able to squash the slightest rumbling of civil disobedience. By January 1941 the strength of the force had been increased from a pre-war level of about 15,000 to more then 23,000 men. Also, from that time, every citizen aged 15 and over had been issued with an ID-card showing his or her photograph and fingerprint, which he or she was obliged to carry at all times.

The Nazis obviously had their own security organisations, with which the Dutch police had been instructed to co-operate. These consisted of the *Ordnungspolizei*, the regular, uniformed police force, commonly known as *Grüne Polizei* or green police after the colour of its uniform; the *Sicherheitspolizei und SD*, the security services; and the *Abwehr*, military intelligence and counter-intelligence.

A co-ordination centre was established in The Hague, run by the SD, which was modelled exactly after the *Reichssicherheitshauptamt* (Central Security Office) in Berlin. Every Berlin *Amt* (office) was mirrored by an *Abteilung* (department) in The Hague and each of these was subdivided into *Referate* (work units), carbon copies of the ones in Berlin. And thus it was that when, in March 1941, Adolf Eichmann established in Berlin the notorious *Referat IV B 4* to oversee the *Endlösung der Judenfrage* (final solution of the Jewish problem), a copycat *Referat IV B 4* was quickly set up in The Hague.

The most senior officer with responsibility for the policing of the occupied Netherlands was *SS-Brigadeführer* (Major-General) Hanns

Albin Rauter, who, shortly after the occupation, had been personally appointed by Himmler, the head of the Gestapo, to the position of *Höhere SS-und Polizeiführer* (CO of SS and Police). Rauter had been groomed in the severely disciplined and centralised system imposed on the German security services by Himmler and his deputy Heydrich and was most uncomfortable with the apparent lack of central control in the Netherlands. In order to bring the Dutch police force - and with it, the Dutch population - more effectively under Nazi control, he even tried to remove the mayors from their traditional position of responsibility for local policing and to impose compulsory training in Nazi ideology on all police officers. While these attempts proved too ambitious, he did ensure that the intelligence services of the local police forces were monitored by trusted local members of the Dutch Nazi party or other Nazi sympathisers.

Both the *Sicherheitspolizei* or Sipo as they were known, and the SD were active in political espionage but only members of Sipo were authorised to make actual arrests. Both services made use of a network of *Vertrauensmänner* (trusted agents) or *V-männer* for short. These were Germans or Dutch citizens, usually members of the Dutch Nazi party, who would pass to the SD any piece of information they would come across which they thought might be useful to the Nazis. These volunteer V-men were everywhere: in offices, pubs, restaurants, cinemas and even in churches where they would take careful note of any anti-German sentiments spoken or even intimated in the sermons. Some V-men were expressly assigned to infiltrate resistance groups. These spies worked on contract and were either paid a fee per item of information or received a fixed SD salary. The most successful V-man, Anton van der Waals, received at least 1,000 Guilders per month, roughly the pre-war salary of a university professor!

THE RESISTANCE TAKES ROOT

However, in spite of all these policing measures, active resistance began to take shape. At first, this only consisted of sabotage, which might involve cutting telephone lines used for German military communications, disrupting production at the Fokker aircraft factory or in shipyards which had been forced to work for the Germans or, indeed, blowing up vital railroad junctions with explosives stolen from German military depots. But the resistance movement soon realised that the effect of these acts was rather short-lived and retaliation from the Germans was harsh and swift and endangered the lives of innocent civilians. Therefore, the emphasis soon shifted to measures which had a more long term effect, like armed raids on distribution centres to obtain bulk food coupons which were essential to support the increasing number of people who had gone underground. The most spectacular of this type of operation was the daring raid, on March 27th 1943, on the Amsterdam municipal archives when vast numbers of files were put to the torch, destroying the means by which the Nazis could locate any citizen of Amsterdam they wanted to lay their hands on. Sometimes, armed attacks were even carried out on prisons in order to free certain vital members of the resistance. Needless to say, the more daring the raid, the greater the risk to the participants, many of whom lost their lives in the effort.

The Nazi administration made life for the Jews progressively more complicated. Orders and prohibitions followed each other in quick succession:

19.12.1940   Germans or people of Germanic origin are no longer allowed to work in Jewish homes.

10.01.1941   All Jews have to register with the authorities (by the end of August more than 160,000 people have complied).

05.02.1941   Jewish professionals are no longer allowed to work for gentiles.

31.05.1941   Jews are no longer allowed to swim in public.

Jews are no longer allowed to enter public parks or buildings, or to rent rooms in hotels, pensions or lodging houses.

Jews are no longer allowed to attend horse races.

15.09.1941 Jews are prohibited from visiting cafés and restaurants including those on stations and in trains, public parks, zoos, theatres, concert halls, cabarets, cinemas, sports facilities, public libraries, reading rooms and museums.

09.05.1942 All Jews must wear a yellow star when outside the home.

June 1942 Jews are only allowed to shop for meat, fish and vegetables in Jewish shops or specially designated markets; they are only allowed into non-Jewish shops between the hours of 3 and 5 p.m.; no purchases can be delivered to Jewish homes; all Jews have to surrender their bicycles before June 24th; all Jews must remain in their homes between 8 p.m. and 6 a.m.

A group of people who successfully resisted Nazi interference in the carrying out of their professional duties were the doctors. When the attempt was made to Nazify the Dutch medical association, 58% of the 5864 members resigned. On September 27th 1941 the entire board resigned. The Germans tried to impose a "Medical Institute", which resulted in a letter of protest signed by 4,261 doctors. The Nazis persisted however, and required all doctors to register on penalty of a fine of 1,000 Guilders. About 1,600 doctors registered, of whom 250 were NSB (*Nationaal Socialistische Beweging* or National Socialist Movement) members and some 600 were Jews who were urged to register by their colleagues because of the extra risk they would run if they refused. In February 1943 the Nazis increased the pressure by starting to fine some doctors 100 guilders for every fortnight they had not registered. A month later the doctors decided to remove their nameplates from their doors: if they were not practising medicine they could not be required to register! This caused great confusion amongst the German administration, as they could not run a country without doctors. Who would sign the death certificates? Eventually they capitulated and the nameplates were put back. A few months later the Nazis again tried to bring the doctors to heel. This time 360 of them were arrested and many doctors now went into hiding, once again causing chaos. Eventually an uneasy truce was established and the doctors were not, as a group, bothered again.

CENSORSHIP

Almost the most disturbing measure the Germans imposed was the strict censorship on the media. The only access to uncensored news was available through the few people who had radios capable of receiving the broadcasts of the BBC from London. Listening to uncensored broadcasts was, of course, strictly forbidden on punishment of confiscation of the equipment and often worse. When it became obvious that not many people took notice of this prohibition, the mere possession of such radios was proscribed which only meant that, very soon, all these wirelesses were carefully hidden in sometimes very imaginative hidey-holes. The news from London was spread by word of mouth and became a very necessary antidote to the Nazi propaganda.

The forced introduction of censors into every newspaper's editing room at the very beginning of the occupation meant that, from then on, the print media had to be considered unreliable. The Nazi propaganda machine attempted to lure the Dutch into collaboration by trying to instil the idea of 'Germanic brother nationhood' and by reporting extensively on the successes of the mighty German army 'which would surely soon defeat all its opponents'.

To counter this, clandestine pamphlets started circulating in which the Dutch were exhorted to ignore the propaganda and take action by joining an underground organisation.

On May 29th 1940, the first pamphlet appeared. It was the work of a 48-year old crafts teacher, Bernard IJzerdraat, who had travelled in Nazi-Germany, had seen what was happening there and had become a rabid anti-Nazi. His idea was to create a network of "sleepers", secret agents who could be activated by the use of passwords. IJzerdraat, unfortunately, had no idea how to safeguard secrecy and security, nor how to mould an underground network out of a bunch of enthusiastic patriots. It did not take the Germans many months to arrest hundreds of people whose only offence was that their name appeared on a membership list of one of these networks. Many were deported to German concentration camps; others were cruelly interrogated and eventually condemned to death by a Nazi court. On March 13th, 1941, eighteen of them were executed somewhere in the dunes near The Hague, the first of many Dutch resistance fighters to be brought before a firing squad.

During the war, quite a number of underground newspapers were to appear which together presented a fairly accurate reflection of the various social, political and religious ideas prevailing in Dutch society at the time. One of the first was produced by a professional journalist, Frans Goedhart, who in July 1940 started to write his "newsletters" under his pseudonym Pieter 't Hoen. These newsletters would eventually become the broadsheet *Het Parool* which would be published right up to the end of the war and was to become the respected newspaper it still is today.

The underground newspapers fulfilled a very important role as they not only provided a more accurate account of the fortunes of war, but also were able to inform the population in advance of German measures and regulations that would affect their daily lives. In addition they tried, of course, to steer public opinion by publishing political essays and columns promoting active resistance and criticizing all forms of collaboration with the enemy. It is estimated that throughout the country about 1,200 broadsheets or bulletins were published during the war, some of them daily. Amsterdam was the centre for the illegal press. Some 150 different publications were produced there. The larger papers had quite considerable circulation figures: *Het Parool*, 60,000; *Trouw* 145,000; *Vrij Nederland* and *De Waarheid*: 100,000.

STARVATION AND THE HUNGER WINTER

Another major impact on daily life was the introduction of food distribution. Pre-war Holland was a prosperous country, its wealth firmly rooted in its well-managed agricultural economy. In addition, it benefited from a large and efficient merchant navy which brought products from its colonies and elsewhere.

Deprived of imports and suffering the forced exports imposed by the Germans, life in the Netherlands became leaner. In July 1940, butter, fat and margarine were rationed, per person, to 500 grams (one Dutch pound) every fortnight; rice, flour, oatmeal and barley each to 125 grams every three weeks; semolina and noodles or cornflour each to 100 grams every seven weeks. In 1941 milk was also rationed, and cocoa rationed to use by children only. By this time the distribution of coffee and tea was discontinued, as neither product was available any more. There was a coffee substitute that was manufactured out of roast flower bulbs and sugar beet and flavoured with chicory but this tasted so foul as to be virtually undrinkable. In the best mercantile tradition, the imposition of food rationing led, of course, to a buoyant black market economy, which persisted throughout the conflict.

As the Nazis immediately began to requisition the Dutch herds to supply the *Wehrmacht* and the German populace, meat rations soon dwindled. By 1943 a ration of meat on the bone had been cut from an initial 200 to a mere 125 grams per person per week. Illegal slaughter was rampant and black market meat, at grossly inflated prices, continued to be available up to the end of the war.

In pre-war Amsterdam, the price of a kilo of prime steak was two Guilders (equivalent to two shillings at the time and 30 British pence today) while pork cost one Guilder 60 cent per kilo. By 1942 prices had risen to four Guilders per kilo for beef, 18 Guilders for lard and one Guilder 50 cent for a kilo of bones. One year later meat prices had gone up to 30 Guilders per kilo while lard and butter were sold for 50 and 60 Guilders per kilo, respectively. A kilo of sugar cost 15 Guilders. A bottle of black market brandy or Dutch gin would set one back 45 to 50 Guilders!

The lowest point came during the terrible winter of 1944–1945, which is known as the 'Hunger Winter'. By this time, virtually all able-bodied men between 16 and 40 years old had either been sent away to hard labour in Germany or were in hiding to escape the German *razzias* or round-ups. The Government-in-Exile in London had called for a railway strike to assist the Allied advances. This brought to a virtual standstill the already poor food supplies to the more industrialised western part of the country. The towns were starving. Bread rations were reduced to 500 grams per person per week. In Amsterdam, 600 people died every week, more than triple the normal number. It was exceptionally cold and coal for cooking and heating was unavailable. Anything that would burn was taken, trees from the park, sleepers from the tram rails and all the wood from the houses left behind by deported Jews. Crowds of starving townspeople of all classes, middle-aged men, women and children, all carrying bags or pushing bicycles with tyres made of wood, prams or makeshift trolleys, went searching for food in the countryside, taking with them anything they had of value to barter with. Sixty-two per cent of all Amsterdam families went on journeys like this. In exchange for their last pieces of clothing, shoes or linen or heirlooms of jewellery or silver, the farmer would let them have some potatoes, peas, beans, tulip bulbs, sugar beet, flour or cheese - anything at all that could be used for food. Up to 50,000 people were on the road at any one time during this terrible winter, all looking for whatever little food was left. How many of them perished from sheer exhaustion can only be guessed at.

It is estimated that about 350,000 people went into hiding, or underground, for shorter or longer periods during the war. These included Jews, resistance activists, men who wanted to avoid the German forced labour camps, shot-down allied air crew and, after the great railway strike in autumn 1944, all 30,000 railway employees! All of these people did not only physically disappear, but also administratively. Special resistance organisations supported these *onderduikers*, literally 'submergers'. Some specialised in finding hiding places in the homes of people brave enough to give shelter; sometimes entire communities would be involved. One group would spirit countless Jewish children away after they had been rounded up by the Nazis. Others would provide safe houses for resistance activists and air crew. Not only did those people have to be hidden away, they had to be fed and cared for. A great many people were involved in stealing or falsifying ration books and distributing them, others offered general support: what to do if somebody fell ill, or if the neighbours got suspicious? Who could help if there was word of an impending *razzia* and whole groups of people would have to be moved to safer places? What if somebody died? Where could you bury them? There are many unsung heroes who risked their lives time and again to help and support this large group of people who had to disappear from normal life.

SOME FACTS AND FIGURES

Pre-war Holland had a population of around 9.5 million people of which about 1.5 per cent or 145,000 were Jews. Most of these lived in Amsterdam and constituted about 15 per cent of that city's total population of 800,000. About 100,000 Jews died in concentration camps and another 10,000 or so died in Holland as a direct result of persecution. It is thought that a total of about 250,000 Dutch people died during the war, roughly 2.5 per cent of the population.

Active organised resistance only started very slowly. It is estimated that, by the summer of 1942, only a few hundred people were involved From spring 1943 the resistance network expanded greatly and throughout the war about 76,000 people were involved in resistance activity either full-time or part-time. Of these, some 24,000 were involved in the underground press, help to allied air crew and the forging of documents; 4,000 in financial activities; 5,000 were active in espionage; 2,000 in armed resistance; some 40,000 were involved in the hiding and housing of *onderduikers:* Jews and others sought by the Nazis. This group saved the lives of some 16,000 Jews, and countless resistance activists, allied pilots and others. When they were caught they and their charges usually paid with their lives. 2,807 resistance activists are known to have been executed in Holland, while some 22,500 did not survive imprisonment or deportation.

Out of 3.5 million townspeople, at least 22,000 starved to death during the Hunger Winter. Relief only came when, in February 1945, the Allied blockade against Germany and German occupied territory was lifted just enough to allow food supplies from neutral Sweden to be air-dropped into the starving Netherlands. Nevertheless, on 18th April 1945, Colonel Henri Koot, based in Amsterdam and in charge of the underground military organisation, sent a telegram to the London government stating that "if liberation is continued at this step by step pace, almost nothing but water will remain".

The Dutch merchant navy played an active role in the war. Some 640 cargo ships and 200 coasters were not in their home ports when Germany invaded the Netherlands, and these were consequently put under the direction of the Government-in-Exile in London and were actively involved in the war effort, such as the trans-Atlantic convoys. Of this fleet, 46 per cent was lost, totalling 387 ships of which 36 were coasters. Out of the some 18,500 crew almost 20 per cent, some 3,600 people, died during the war.

In October 1945, the Dutch government provided the British government with a breakdown, in pre-war prices, of the cost of the damage done to the country by the Germans. It contained the following (in million guilders):

	Guilders million
Damage due to war action	5,390
Public property commandeered or stolen	3,640
Losses due to failure to improve production apparatus	2,390
Losses to industry: real estate, machinery and stocks	2,000
Losses to trade: real estate and stock	1,800
Losses to merchant fleet	325
Losses to port installations	300
Losses to public transport	680
Damage to roads and bridges	100
Damage to agricultural land (forced inundations and airfield construction)	825
Loss of personal property (including everything confiscated from Jews, one million commandeered bicycles and 600,000 wirelesses.)	1,200
Gold, currencies and valuables	2,850
Damage to private real estate (100,000 homes destroyed and 50,000 severely damaged)	1,000
	22,500

In today's terms 278 billion guilders or 89 billion pounds.

CONTENTS

I

PRELUDE

BEFORE IT ALL BEGAN

I was born in Bandung, Java, in 1916 and lived in the former Dutch East Indies until my father, a civil servant, was pensioned off early in 1933 in the wake of the economic depression. We repatriated to Amsterdam where I finished school and went to university to study medicine in 1935. Perhaps partly as a result of growing up in a colonial society, I had little interest in politics and took government for granted. It never really occurred to me that all over Europe authoritarian ideologies had become rather en vogue, nor that dictators like Mussolini and Franco were quietly applauded for crushing the power of the leftwing trade-unions in their country at the expense of parliamentary democracy. It had not struck me either that when Hitler, on the back of blatantly rigged elections, assumed power in Germany, only a few perceptive people appeared to be aware of the menace to peace, nor that horrendous stories about concentration camps in which the Nazis starved and tortured their political adversaries were often dismissed as communist propaganda. I was about to get a rude awakening.

Following the outrage of the destruction of synagogues and other Jewish property during the notorious *Kristallnacht* (Night of Broken

3

Glass), which took place all over Germany at the instigation of the Nazis in November 1938, Jewish friends of mine asked me to go, at their expense, and see some of their relatives in Germany to find out if they were all right. I made four trips and saw with my own eyes how the Nazis were systematically persecuting and harassing a group of citizens, ordinary German businessmen, manufacturers, artists, scientists or whomever, not for political reasons but just because they had one or more grandparents whom the Nazis looked upon as *Untermenschen* (sub-humans). This shameless display of racism turned me into a confirmed enemy of the Nazis there and then and it made me eager to help its victims in any way I could. Some of the Jews were anxious to get at least their portable valuables out of Germany. Not only were they afraid of the rampant looting of Jewish property but many had also applied for permission to emigrate and knew that they would certainly never get permission to take their property with them. They therefore asked me if I would be willing to take some of their things with me back to Holland. It did vaguely occur to me that this might well be a bit risky, but to think about being sensible in the face of so much desperation seemed horribly trite.

On my last trip back I carried five suitcases stuffed with family jewellery, fur coats and other valuables, and also the latest Leitz binocular microscope which belonged to a German refugee friend of mine. The only other passenger in my compartment was a middle-aged man who had watched me goggle-eyed board the train with all my luggage. Speaking German, he asked me jokingly whether I was emigrating. I said that I was a student and had brought last term's dirty laundry to have it washed at home during the Christmas holidays. This shut him up most effectively.

However, the closer we got to the Dutch border the more nervous my travelling companion seemed to get. He took to pacing the corridor and looked at me with obvious bemusement. He clearly could not make me out. I went to the lavatory and had to pass him in the corridor. Out of the blue he asked me if I could possibly look after his suitcase and claim it as mine at Customs control.

As the pressure on my bladder did not allow me the luxury of thought, I rashly agreed. He then simply handed me his keys and I did not see him again until after we had crossed the border.

German Customs were no problem. They could tell from my passport that I was a student and swallowed my story about going home for the holidays rather than bother to check my luggage. But the Dutch were never so easygoing and asked me to open four of my bags for inspection. To give myself time to think I did not exactly rush it. How was a shabby and penniless student going to account for five suitcases full of treasure, not to mention the highly dutiable Leitz! While I was still busy fiddling and fumbling with locks and keys, the officer asked me if I had anything to declare. I shook my head, but then reconsidered and earnestly told him about an old portable typewriter I had with me and whether I should not perhaps have to pay duty on that. He looked at the time-worn machine and asked me what I had paid for it. As it had been given to me by the owner of the suitcase I was just unlocking, I could tell him, truthfully, that it was a present. He then asked me what it was worth and when I said I had no idea he sent me to the Customs office to have it valued.

As I picked up the typewriter and made to do as I was told, he said that I had better first re-lock my suitcases if I did not want to find myself robbed on my return. I thanked him for his concern, locked the bags and went out onto the platform to find the Customs office. I joined the queue and, by being deliberately over-polite, managed to stay at the end of it. This way, at least, I kept myself out of the orbit of the inquisitive customs officer. When it was finally my turn, I had to pay 2.75 guilders import duty as the typewriter had been manufactured in Germany. I did not argue as, by that time, the stationmaster had just blown his whistle and the train was already moving. I leapt on, safe in the knowledge that the Customs officers would have left it seconds earlier.

I returned the keys to my "fostered" suitcase to their rightful owner who accepted them with speechless gratitude and then, without a word of explanation, disappeared. I never did find out what it was this strange bird had had me smuggle into the country.

And so I journeyed on to Amsterdam with my precious luggage unmolested and a little time to consider the lessons that could be learned from this experience: never panic, make use of any lucky break and put your trust in being smarter than anything in uniform.

In 1939, when war broke out and there was general mobilisation in Holland, I had just finished military service primary training for medical officers. As, however, the Army had no use for unqualified personnel, the conscript medical students were garrisoned in their respective university towns and told to continue their studies.

In Amsterdam our quarters were in a commandeered hostel for homeless and juvenile delinquents on Lauriergracht. All we had to do was to attend roll call in the morning and clean the dorms, but other than that nobody bothered us with military exercises or discipline. We were required to attend regularly our lectures at university and we had to sign an attendance list every time we were there. This meant that an assiduous student like me soon became very adept in the forging of signatures, which would prove to be quite an asset in the future.

THE FIVE-DAY WAR

On May 10th, 1940, we were rudely woken at 4 a.m. as German planes bombed the airport at Schiphol. In the ensuing pandemonium, the Command of the Army Medical Corps apparently had completely forgotten about the existence of us conscript medical students and nobody seemed to know what to do with us. After a lot of confusion we were all put on transport to The Hague and dropped, perhaps appropriately, on Tournament Square, to await further orders.

We waited, and waited, and waited, feeling useless and totally superfluous in the middle of all the confusion of a war of which the only evidence we saw was the odd German Ju 52 paratroop transport flying over. We cheered loudly when one was occasionally hit by our anti-aircraft batteries or shot down by one of the very few Dutch fighters still in the air.

Eventually we were marched off to a nearby empty school where we had to move the desks before we could put down some army pallets. And again we waited and waited, with nothing to do but while away the time with cards. Wild rumours took us from exuberant optimism to utter despair: British commandos had arrived in Rotterdam; breaching the dikes had stopped the German advance; the fifth column had attacked the Dutch HQ; French troops were gaining ground in Zeeland; there were German paratroopers in disguise, wearing Dutch uniforms and even nuns' habits; the Government had sent the Royal Family to England, and so on.

On the 14th of May we were told that the German air force, Goering's "glorious" *Luftwaffe*, had savagely bombed and destroyed the ancient centre of the city of Rotterdam and in the face of Nazi threats to do the same elsewhere, the Dutch army had capitulated.

That night we were sent by bus to Rotterdam to give aid to victims of the bombing. But as nobody seemed to know what good a busload of medical students could do in the blazing city, we spent the night being driven from pillar to post through clouds of smoke and soot until we were ordered back to The Hague at daybreak, feeling tired, filthy and utterly useless.

The normally busy road, then the only dual carriage-way in the country, was virtually empty of traffic but littered with the ghastly debris of war.

We saw some German tanks littering the verge of the road and their dead-beat crew fast asleep by their side. We saw wrecks of German aeroplanes scattered in fields between dead cows and horses with bloated bellies and stiff legs pointing skyward in silent protest. And for the first time in our life we saw corpses of soldiers killed in action. The sight of the Dutch boys filled us with outrage, that of the Germans only with grim satisfaction.

My friend Mau Frenkel was sitting next to me in the bus and still vividly remembers being so overwhelmed by the overall devastation that he muttered: "This is the end for Holland!", and also my reply: "No, it isn't, we will just have to fight to get our country back!".

This futile mission of mercy was the sum total of our stint in the army. The next day we were sent back to Amsterdam where we were soon demobilised, free to go home and resume our studies.

II

THE OCCUPATION

THE VELVET GLOVE

The first few weeks of Nazi occupation were a time of great confusion. Lots of conflicting rumours were circulating. This was made even worse by the propaganda and press censorship of the Germans. People were feeling abandoned by the government and by their beloved queen who had gone into exile. Some were relieved that the German soldiers appeared to be disciplined and did not rape, loot and pillage as they were said to have done in Poland. There were, of course, the inevitable black-outs and the occasional flak guns firing at British reconnaissance planes, but otherwise pretty soon life seemed to go on as usual. Little did we know what misery the Nazis still had in store for us!

Immediately after the Dutch capitulation the *Wehrmacht* established a military administration. However Hitler, who never trusted his generals, posted the freshly appointed *Militärbefehlshaber* (military commandant) General Alexander von Falkenhausen, a Right Wing aristocrat but not a Nazi, to the High Command in Belgium and Northern France after only nine days in The Netherlands. In his stead the *Führer* appointed as *Reichskommissar für die besetzten niederländischen Gebiete* (Governor of the occupied Low Countries) a shrewd Austrian lawyer, Arthur Seyss-Inquart, who had earned Hitler's trust by providing him with the legal arguments for the taking over of Austria in 1938, the so-called *Anschluss*.

The Netherlands, with their economic wealth and rich colonies, were a prize that Hitler badly wanted. He tried to pull the wool over our eyes by calling us a "brother nation" and deserving of the special honour of incorporation into his *Grossgermanisches Reich* (Greater German Empire). It was for this reason that the Netherlands was the only occupied country to be ruled by a civil administration (different from Norway, but that was for another reason). But there was to be a high price to be paid for this dubious distinction. In the other occupied countries the military were in command and for them the persecution of Jews was not a priority. This meant that any zeal in this area was usually counterbalanced by the desire of the military administration to avoid public unrest. But Holland was ruled by a committed Nazi, whose priorities were political rather than military and this meant that a disproportionately high number of Dutch Jews would eventually be deported.

Hitler's instructions to Seyss-Inquart were that he should only slowly and gradually try to convert the Dutch people to national-socialism and to avoid as long as possible any measures in areas known to be sensitive, such as religion or anti-Jewish regulations. In a clumsy attempt to try and win the Dutch around, Hitler authorized Seyss-Inquart to announce the release of all Dutch POWs on the day he was installed in office. This "magnanimous gesture of the Führer", however, singularly failed to impress the Dutch. They did not have a high opinion of Seyss-Inquart, in rhyming slang soon known as *Zes-en-een-kwart* (six and a quarter); to them he was just a bloody traitor who had delivered his country up to Hitler. The Dutch, never known for their subtlety, did not hide their feelings and soon the Germans were said to grumble: "The Czechs shoot at us, the Poles spit at us, but the Dutch simply cut us dead!"

This was actually very true. Blacked-out Amsterdam, with its many canals, was a dangerous place for the unwary. Even a local, especially when in a certain – or rather uncertain – state would sometimes stagger into the drink. The splash and the cry for help would bring a jeering but helpful crowd out into the street and somebody would always quickly and effectively wield the boathook affixed to every bridge for just such an occasion. However, when the cry was *"Hilfe!"*, the people of Amsterdam were curiously struck with a sudden deafness and many an unfortunate German was left to flounder and figure out how to scale a perpendicular brick canal wall covered in about 300 years of slime. He could count himself very fortunate if, in the nick of time, a voice would suddenly come out of the dark and enquire solicitously if he was managing all right.

Meanwhile, the German war machine was rolling on and brought disaster upon disaster: the Belgians capitulated a fortnight after the Dutch and the French followed suit on June 22nd. But the British miraculously managed to withdraw the bulk of their expeditionary force from Dunkirk and the Dutch were much heartened by their brave resolution to continue the struggle on their own and try to defeat the Nazis.

The mood of confidence inspired by the British resolve, as expressed in Churchill's eloquent speeches, also gave rise to a spontaneous nation-wide demonstration of loyalty to the Dutch Crown on June 29th. This was the birthday of Prince Bernhard of Lippe-Biesterfeld who, in 1937, had married Crown Princess Juliana. In celebration, national and orange flags were flown, bunches of flowers were heaped on the doorsteps of the Royal palaces and around statues of members of the House of Orange. Many people also wore the white carnation button hole without which Prince Bernhard was never seen. The Nazi administration was completely taken by surprise and, as Seyss-Inquart happened to be away on a working visit in the north of The Netherlands, they were at a loss as to how to react. When furious members of the Dutch Nazi party began tearing the white carnations off the coats of passers-by, some demonstrators deftly slipped a razorblade behind the carnation which, most satisfactorily, resulted in a lot of these petty Nazi activists ending up with their own blood on their hands.

When the news reached Hitler, he became so incensed that he summoned Seyss-Inquart and General Christiansen, the *Wehrmachtsbefehlshaber in den Niederländen* (Military Commander in The Netherlands) to his headquarters. They eventually assured Hitler that the reports were grossly exaggerated and that the severe reprisals he had in mind were unnecessary as the situation was fully under control. They told him that General Winkelman, Commander-in-Chief of the Dutch army, had been arrested on the 1st July at dead of night and had been deported to Germany; that the Mayor of The Hague had been dismissed for failing to stop people laying flowers at the doors of the Royal Palace and that the press had been instructed never to mention any member of the Royal family again. Little did they realise that it was a delusion to think that this was going to bring the Dutch around!

In September 1940 I discovered by chance, on the Prinsengracht in Amsterdam, an abandoned and rather dilapidated 18th-century mews of almshouses, called *"Het Nieuwe Suyckerhofje"* (The New Sugar Mews). The last of the old ladies had moved out in 1937 and it had been vacant ever since. It was going for such a low rent that two friends of mine and I decided to take it and live there. The mews had been built on some of the gardens that backed onto each other between the houses on the Prinsengracht and Keizersgracht and consisted of five tiny three-storeyed houses and a chapel. It seemed appropriate to establish there the "Order of the Prince's Monks" with Herman Maillette de Buy Wenniger (who had both the aristocratic name and the looks to fit the post) as Prior and Emil Sindram and myself as Canons (of Practical and Impractical Matters, respectively).

We soon gathered an exclusive small band of tenants, each of whom had to submit to a rather gruelling dinner-party presided over by the Prior who would, after entering into private conclave with his brethren, not hesitate to blackball any of the hopefuls whose table or other manners and mannerisms offended his sensibilities. Each new tenant was given a set of our House Rules to which they had to swear obedience in a solemn ceremony. In a way we established a commune *avant-la-lettre*, which soon matured into a nucleus of anti-Nazi activity. One strict rule was that, for security reasons, each and every resident was responsible for keeping the entrance-gate locked shut at all times.

Meanwhile, the Nazi administration gradually tightened its grip. In October 1940 it was decreed that civil servants were to file a declaration of Aryan origin. As I was of the opinion that my grandparents' origin was nobody's business I refused, with the result that I was promptly dismissed from my job as student-assistant at the Municipal University of Amsterdam. One month later, the Nazis dismissed all Jewish professors and teachers.

The infamy of this anti-Jewish decree incited Professor Cleveringa, a professor of law in Leiden, to hold a brilliant lecture to protest against this blatant violation of academic freedom, which had also caused the dismissal of the man who had been his own tutor, the internationally renowned lawyer Professor E.M. Meijers. His passionate words of abhorrence and indignity struck a spark in the packed auditorium and this led to a massive student strike whereupon the Germans closed the ancient University of Leiden which was not to re-open till after the war. Two days later Prof. Cleveringa was arrested and kept in custody for eight months.

At Amsterdam University some of us made a fervent appeal to our fellow-students to follow suit, but this was blocked by the Rector Magnificus, Professor B. Brouwer, who addressed the protesting crowd and promised that he would try and come to an arrangement with the German authorities which, of course, was a sham.

JOINING THE RESISTANCE

As I keenly felt the treachery of the unprovoked attack of the German army on our country, and even more the systematic desecration of our liberties and democratic institutions by the Nazi regime, I wanted to escape to England and join the Allied forces. Early in 1941 I was introduced to a journalist, Lex Althoff, who was said to be able to help me realise my plan. Only after the war I learned how dangerous this "help" might have been: many people as green and naive as I was, took this route only to blunder straight into the web of the notorious traitor Anton Van der Waals and end up in a German prison or worse. Lex, unknowingly, was being used by this infamous *V-mann* as a stoolpigeon in the *Englandspiel*, until he himself was arrested in May 1942 and later executed by the Nazis.

When I told him that I wanted to join the British forces, Lex convinced me that I could fight the Nazis more directly and effectively by joining the Resistance at home, and introduced me to a colleague of his, Frans Goedhart, who needed help with stencilling and distribution of an underground weekly *Het Parool* (The Word of Honour).

Frans Goedhart was a remarkable and gifted journalist who, as early as 1933, had recognised the threat of Nazi Germany to European democracy and to the independence of the Netherlands. In July 1940, under his *nom de plume* Pieter 't w, he started to write and distribute an underground newsletter in which he mercilessly attacked everyone who either sided, collaborated or even came to terms with the policy of the Nazis. He fiercely condemned any form of political activity except for underground resistance on the grounds that anything else was, in fact, collaboration with the enemy.

The quality of these newsletters soon attracted the attention of like-minded people, amongst them the former chairman of the SDAP (Dutch Labour party), Koos Vorrink, who offered Goedhart his many contacts in the socialist youth organisation to help him distribute the newsletters nationwide.

In the autumn of 1940 it was agreed to replace the newsletter with a regular weekly newspaper, still underground of course, to be named: *Het Parool*. The editors were: Frans Goedhart, Koos Vorrink, Lex Althoff, Maurits Kann, Hans Warendorf and Jaap Nunes Vaz.

I was to help Frans Goedhart run off the stencilled copies and prepare them for distribution or mail them in hand-addressed envelopes. At first we worked from an office in St. Nicolaas Street, which belonged to Lex Althoff's brother Eduard who had a business distributing fashion magazines. We were soon joined by Jan Stallinga who had been recommended to us by Koos Vorrink as being discreet, diligent and trustworthy, all of which he was and a nice comrade to boot!

Two or three nights every week the three of us slaved happily away at the stencilling machine until at last, in August 1941, a printer was found who was willing to risk his neck and print *Het Parool*. From then on the editors concentrated on editing while Jan and I did the legwork between editor, type setter and printer, as well as handling delivery and distribution of the copies. We all knew that the penalty for being caught was almost certain death.

As in all resistance work, our job required circumspection and imagination. To avoid raising undue suspicion at the Post Office, the addresses were written in different handwritings, we used envelopes of various sizes and colours and mailed them from several locations. We also hand-delivered copies in our own neighbourhood. As we could not always finish before curfew, we often took home the remaining copies to have them distributed later through an ever growing network of volunteers. Needless to say, my trusty friends at the Nieuwe Suyckerhofje also did their share. But however careful we were, novice underground activists like us still needed all the luck we could get.

One day I was on my way to the house of my girlfriend, Saartje Oudkerk, carrying my briefcase and a shopping bag full of things which her family, being Jewish, were no longer allowed to buy. Stupidly

I left my briefcase behind in the tram. Not only did it have my name and address inside, but also copies of *Het Parool* and half a pound of butter, a priceless commodity at the time. I could only hope for the best. To my great relief and surprise my briefcase was delivered to my address some days later with an anonymous note inside. Apparently what had happened was that a passenger in the tram had noticed how a man in the uniform of the WA (the quasi-military branch of the Dutch Nazi party) picked up the briefcase and looked inside. At the terminus he got out, hid the briefcase in some shrubs and rushed off with the butter. Thinking this rather odd, the passenger retrieved the briefcase and found the copies of *Het Parool* inside. He assumed that probably the WA-man had only gone to take the precious butter home and would soon return to collect the briefcase with its incriminating contents and deliver it to the SD like the good little Nazi he undoubtedly was. Not thinking much of this scenario, my unknown benefactor then took the briefcase, distributed the copies of *Het Parool* amongst some trustworthy friends and sent the case back to me. A most chastening lesson and not one I was likely to forget!

Another time that the gods were with me was on a wintry evening in 1941. It had been snowing heavily and the snow had been swept up into big drifts. Once again I was on my way to my girlfriend, by bicycle this time, and carrying a pile of copies of *Het Parool* in my briefcase. Suddenly I was caught up in a *razzia* by the German police. In their usual charming way they told me to get off my bike and line up with some others who had been rounded up earlier. I put my bicycle against a tree and managed to bury my briefcase in a heap of snow. Eventually about thirty of us were marched off to the SD headquarters in the nearby Euterpe Street, where we were searched and interrogated. I unobtrusively let the others go first and so managed to be the last one to be called in.

Of course, the SD did not find anything on me except my I.D. and student card. They asked me what subject I was reading and why I was so far from home. I replied that I was a medical student and had been on my way to a colleague to borrow his lecture notes. The interrogator then asked me if I knew *"die Zeitschrift Die Parole"* (the newspaper *Het Parool*). With what I hoped was my most guileless look I told him that I had never heard of any medical journal by that name, whereupon he barked: *"Sie! Ein Medizinstudent!? Sie sind ja blöd! So einer würde in Deutschland nicht mal zum Medizinstudium zugelassen werden!"* (You! A medical student!? You are an idiot! In Germany somebody this thick would not even be admitted to medical school!). To confirm him in his happy opinion of me, I asked him if he could kindly give me a permit to be out after curfew, as otherwise I could not get home without breaking the German regulations. For a moment he looked at me with speechless disbelief but then, with a sigh, actually gave me a pass. I thanked him graciously, took off, fetched my bike, dug my briefcase out of the snow and, protected by my pass from further molestation, leisurely went about my business distributing the copies of *"Die Parole"*.

For the first time I had faced the lion in his den and I had lived to tell the tale!

THE FEBRUARY STRIKE

Meanwhile, the Nazis took, bit by bit, further measures against the Jews. As long as these were strictly administrative regulations and not accompanied by open violence, they were tolerated as an idiosyncrasy of German rule. The Nazis were, of course, badly put out that the Dutch public did not show more sympathy for their campaign against the Jews, but Seyss-Inquart still continued to tread as carefully as he could, as particularly instructed by Hitler.

This careful policy was, however, badly upset by the NSB (Dutch Nazi party) who started to rattle their sabres as they felt that the time had come to prove themselves. They had never managed to become a political force in Holland and even the leaders of the German Nazis thought of them as a party of clowns with a fool for a leader, all busy trying to ape the real thing. In the beginning of 1941, the NSB sent their uniformed bully-boys into working-class neighbourhoods to harass the Jews living there. The close-knit community of Amsterdam labourers, an excitable bunch at the best of times, was not going to take this lying down! One member of the NSB found himself in the wrong place at the wrong time when he was spotted strutting and taunting down the quarter's main street. He was grabbed by a few sturdy lads who dangled him, upside down, from the nearest bridge. The unfortunate, in fear of his life, screamed and pleaded: "Please don't drown me! I am not a dog, after all!" The men then dropped him in the canal for being a member of the NSB and hauled him out again for promising that he would stop being a dog! There were many incidents like this, such as the mussel vendor whose Nazi slogans offended the locals so much that they simply picked him up, cart, mussels and all and dumped the whole lot into the nearest canal; or the NSB man who thought it safe to shout abuse from a second floor window, only to find his door being kicked in, his belongings reduced to tinder and himself in hospital for a good many weeks.

In February one of the bullies was killed in a similar riot and the NSB went whining to the Germans for support, but in vain! The Head of the SD, *SS-Brigadeführer* (lieutenant-colonel) Hanns Rauter, who had been appointed by Himmler himself, was quite happy to see the NSB disgrace themselves and pointed out that he did not favour having Wild-West scenes in Amsterdam.

A few days later, however, the German Security police had been tipped that a particular ice-cream parlour run by two German Jewish refugees served as a meeting centre for resistance activists and decided to raid the place after closing time. As bad luck would have it, there were indeed a few members of an assault party in the ice-cream parlour when the German policemen knocked on the door. The guys inside could not see who was knocking and assumed it was the NSB. Welcoming the chance of giving these turncoats a memorable reception, they released the vent on a bottle of ammonia and fled through the backdoor to the neighbours. When the Germans had kicked in the door, the corrosive vapour made them recoil and they fired their guns at random in fury and frustration. They had to wait for the air to clear before they could enter, only to find that the birds had flown. Unfortunately, the tracks in the snow-covered garden led them straight to the neighbours where they arrested the culprits.

This incident was played up considerably in the Nazi press, which made it impossible for Rauter to ignore the open opposition of the Amsterdam Jews and their friends to the harassment they suffered at the hands of the NSB. On his instruction the SD now carried out the first *razzias* on Jews. Some four hundred Jewish men and boys were rounded up, savagely beaten and eventually deported to Mauthausen, a notorious German concentration camp where a few months later virtually all of them had died.

The people of Amsterdam were so outraged by this brutal assault on their Jewish neighbours: "The effing Krauts should keep their effing hands off our effing Jews!" that a one-day general strike was called on February 25th, 1941. To the incredulity of the Nazi administration this call was answered in vast numbers. Almost every municipal public service, but also many private factories, saw people down tools. One shop after another closed its doors and soon thousands of people were marching in the streets, shouting slogans protesting the anti-Jewish policy of the Nazis and singing national or socialist marching songs. German soldiers and WA-men in uniform wisely kept well away. The strike spread to other towns and it was not till the next day before the Nazis could put an end to it. This was the only spontaneous demonstration of solidarity with the Jewish population in all of occupied Europe!

Although the strike gave the Dutch an opportunity to vent their frustration with the Nazi occupation, it did mean the end of Seyss-Inquart's kid glove policy with the Dutch!

THE STUDENTS' PROTEST

In spite of the iron hand with which the February strike had been squashed, there continued to be rumblings of discontent as, for instance, amongst the Amsterdam students. In October 1941 Professor Van Apeldoorn, a professor of law at Amsterdam University and a fervent Nazi, was unwise enough to try and teach his students that Hitler's decree to appoint Seyss-Inquart as *Reichskommissar* in The Netherlands was completely in accordance with international war regulations. His audience burst out laughing, and he got so angry that he reported one of the students to the Rector Magnificus and demanded that he be expelled from the University for having insulted the *Führer*. He also threatened to pass on the student's name to the German authorities. The Rector alerted the Dean of the Law Faculty, Professor Hazewinkel-Suringa, who wrote her Nazi colleague a stiff letter in which she pointed out that, as The Netherlands were actually at war with Germany, any Dutch citizen who delivered another into the hands of the enemy was in fact a traitor. Meanwhile another student had sent Professor Van Apeldoorn a sharp letter to protest against his flagrant misinterpretation of the law. Van Apeldoorn now lodged a formal complaint with the Rector in the presence of the newly appointed pro-German Mayor of Amsterdam, E.J. Voûte. Both implored him not to report the incidents to the German authorties. But Van Apeldoorn would not listen and as a result both students were summoned by the SD for a dressing down.

The Nazis now also had the perfect excuse for a thorough political clean-up of Amsterdam University. In January 1942 Professor Hazewinkel-Suringa and six other professors whose loyalty to the German policy was suspect were summoned to The Hague for a long political interrogation. But then a bomb exploded in the building of the Dutch Nazi student society, whereupon Seyss-Inquart ordered that five of the professors, including Hazewinkel-Suringa, as well as ten students were to be arrested and sent to a concentration camp. Even the pro-German secretary of the department of Education, Science and Culture, Professor J. van Dam, protested against this measure, while the Rector Magnificus, Professor B. Brouwer – the same who in December 1940 had foiled the students' attempt to close the University of Amsterdam – consulted the University Senate

When the majority in the Senate took the view that closing the University had now become unavoidable, Brouwer objected, protesting that he would rather take full responsibility himself and declared that he would even deliver himself up to the German authorities to try and prevent closure of the university. But, as the arrests were not carried out, Brouwer's grandiose gesture was never put to the test.

Two days later some further acts of sabotage were carried out in Amsterdam, and the Nazis took dozens of hostages, including three students and five professors, and packed them off to the concentration camp at Amersfoort. When Van Dam protested again at the commotion in his backyard, Seys-Inquart tuttutted that the arrests were only carried out as part of a security sweep in which quite a few prominent people had been detained, but that it was not at all aimed specifically at Amsterdam University. This explanation gave Brouwer the excuse to back down and, again, do nothing.

In fury, some of us, students and resistance activists, tried again to organise a strike to get the University closed. But this time we got very little response as, after the closure of Leiden University, many students had come to Amsterdam to continue their studies and were not eager to support us. Eventually, forty of us sent an open letter to the Rector Magnificus in which we accused him and the Senate of the University of Amsterdam of betraying the traditional principles of academic freedom and tolerance. The Rector Magnificus then summoned each of us individually and required us to withdraw the accusation or face expulsion. I was one of those who refused to recant and, as a result, got a lot more free time to spend on resistance activities. Fortunately, I had just passed my finals!

Meanwhile, in January 1942 Frans Goedhart was caught in an attempt to escape to England.

This was, of course, a terrible blow to our group. Should the publication of *Het Parool* be continued? Vorrink and Althoff wanted to discontinue *Het Parool* and, instead, distribute news bulletins on an ad hoc basis under different names. Hans Warendorf and Jaap Nunes Vaz were of the opinion that not going on would only prove to the Nazis that Frans Goedhart was indeed the much wanted editor of *Het Parool*. Moreover, Frans had arranged that, if something were to happen to him on his trip across the Channel, three friends of Nunes Vaz, Jan Meijer, Cees de Groot and Wim van Norden, would join *Het Parool* as editors. So it was decided that we would go on. Jaap Nunes Vaz was to write leading articles in the style of Pieter 't Hoen, while Jan Stallinga and I remained in charge of the coordination between the editors and the printer and the distribution of the copies.

Our resolve to continue meant that Koos Vorrink and Lex Althoff both decided to withdraw from *Het Parool*.

III

THE 'MINDERS'

OSTRICHES

In August 1942, two Jewish friends of mine, Mau and Siet Frenkel, both medical students, told me that they were planning to escape the tightening vice of Nazi persecution by trying to get to Switzerland. How they had come to this decision is best told in Mau's own words:

Early in 1941 my cousin Sven had been caught in a razzia by the Nazis (read: the Amsterdam police!). In July, a postcard arrived from the concentration camp Mauthausen, on which in shaky handwriting: "I wish for uncle Franz!" (our G.P.). In November 1941 came the report of his death.

We, like ostriches, buried our heads in the sand and thought: "This won't happen to us". Yet, just to be on the safe side, we always carried a vial of potassium cyanide crystals which we had easy access to at the hospital laboratory. If the Germans were going to get us, at least we would deny them the pleasure of getting us alive. A most comforting thought.

The Director of the Binnengasthuis (an Amsterdam teaching hospital) where I worked as Houseman, was a fervent supporter of the Nazi racist ideology. He decreed that Jewish staff had to wear the compulsory yellow star on their white coats. As the local patients could not care less whether or not they were treated by Jewish doctors, this actually was not a big deal. But my next assignment was to the department of dermatology and venereal diseases which was full of hookers with V.D. who were there for compulsory treatment under Wehrmacht rules. These working girls, who knew very well which side their bread was buttered, were not at all shy to voice their opinion and did so in a choice of words that would have put even the most rabid Nazi sailor to the blush. This eventually led to my move to the Jewish Hospital at Nieuwe Prinsengracht. But we still kept our heads in the sand.

In the meantime, the razzias continued. One evening in early August 1942, after curfew, the doorbell rang and we all thought they had come to get us. However, it was not the Grüne Polizei (as the German Police was called, after the colour of their uniform), but Lien van Beverwijk, a friend of my fiancée and active in the Resistance. She was a psychiatry resident and, as such, had a pass allowing her to be out after curfew. She came to warn us and said we should try and leave the country as soon as possible because the latest intelligence she had received was rather alarming.

For ostriches like us, this was hard to swallow! To suddenly have to leave parents, friends and colleagues, a much loved career, one's patients and one's home! Nevertheless, we promised to meet Lien the next day at her flat. And in the morning, as if to confirm the urgency of her message, we received two green pre-printed cards, one for me and one for my brother, ordering us to report with rucksack, flask and toothbrush for a workdetail in Poland! Was signed: Aus der Fünten, SS-Hauptsturmführer. That afternoon Lien introduced us to a man with a straight mousy hair, worn quite long in the singular fashion of artists and mathematicians. His face was pale, his voice had the soft tones of the southern provinces. He wore a beige suit and hornrimmed glasses. This was Mathieu van den Berg. We quickly came to business. First of all we urgently needed proper passport photographs. The photographer turned out to be a nice, plump and bald middle-aged man who had been a doctor in pre-Hitler Germany but now lived in an attic somewhere in Amsterdam where he took photographs for forged I.D. cards. We also had to lay our hands on some funds, as not everybody who was involved in our escape did so out of friendship and humanitarian motives. My parents had no income other than the unemployment *benefit of my father who had been dismissed from his teaching post by the Nazis. Lien offered to go and negotiate on our behalf with "the Golden Calf", a wealthy uncle of ours in The Hague who had acquired his nickname because money seemed to love him quite as much as he loved money. But Lien got what she wanted, and final arrangements for our journey were made. On August 17th my brother and I went to pay our respects to the parents of two sweet little cousins of ours who had just been caught in a razzia and would never come back. This visit finally made us take our heads out of the sand!*

SO FAR MAU FRENKEL'S STORY.

It had been arranged that the Frenkels would meet Mathieu van den Berg at the station restaurant in Roosendaal, a town near the Dutch-Belgian border. Mathieu would then take them to people who would, in turn, smuggle them across the border and instruct them how to find their next contact.

Deeply worried by his sons' precarious plans, father Frenkel, whom I liked very much, had suffered a heart attack. To alleviate his anxiety, I promised him privately to keep a close eye on things.

The Frenkels were to spend the night before their departure in "Het Nieuwe Suyckerhofje" as, in view of the curfew, it would be easier the next day for them to get to the Central Station from there than from their own home. In the afternoon of the 18th of August Mau and Siet came to my place, where they removed from their coats the ignominious yellow stars which the Nazis made it compulsory for Jews to wear. As their identity cards, stamped with the mandatory capital "J", branded them as Jews, I gave them new I.D. cards. These actually were legally issued documents lifted from the convenient supply of jackets always on hand in the hospital junior-registrars' changing room. All I had to do was to replace the photographs and apply some of my drawing skills to the reproduction of the official stamp. Germans are great believers in official looking stamps!

I also made the Frenkels memorise the name, address, and telephone number of Daan and Cox van der Putten, friends of mine in Brussels who might be useful to them.

The next morning I accompanied them to the Central Station and saw them safely on the train to Roosendaal. I then, without their knowledge, took a seat in a different carriage of the same train, in order to fulfil my promise to their father. At Roosendaal station I saw, from a discreet distance, how they met their man and walked off with him. As I was never keen on pedestrian locomotion, I rented a bicycle at the station and followed them at a distance until I saw them enter a house at the edge of town. When, after about an hour, they had not re-emerged, I decided they must have left through the backdoor.

It was a beautiful summerday with a clear blue sky and I thought I might quite enjoy a ride in the general direction of the Belgian border in the hope of catching a glimpse of them. Small country roads led me through fields with golden corn and orchards full of ripening fruit. The world seemed totally at peace and war only a bad dream.

Suddenly I came upon a provincial road where, to my surprise, I saw a Belgian signpost pointing to Essen, a small town across the border from Roosendaal. Without anybody, myself included, being any the wiser I had obviously crossed the border! I followed the signpost and duly arrived in Essen where I found a little café with a view of the railway station. As I supposed my friends were also heading here, I took a seat on the terrace. I cursed the fact that I had no Belgian money, which meant that I could not even buy myself a lovely cool Belgian lager which I was dying for!

A little later my friends indeed arrived, on foot, in the company of an elderly lady and a young man whom they had met in the house in Roosendaal. I had rightly assumed that they had left through the backdoor, and they had bicycled to the border, probably over the very same small road I had found, with a twelve year old boy as their guide. At the border they had left the bicycles and my lovely handcrafted

Dutch I.D. cards with the boy and got forged Belgian papers in return. They were told to wait for their *passeur* (see note 1) at the bus stop. But the *passeur* failed to show and they eventually decided to try and make it to Essen on their own. They were, of course, greatly startled to find me there.

The elderly lady was so excited by her adventure and the success of her first step on the road to liberty, that she treated us all to an ice-cream, at the time an untold luxury. But her unabated excitement was so apparent that she started to attract far too much attention. It seemed not to have occurred to her that, in our situation, unobtrusiveness was imperative. Anyway, I thought it advisable to relieve ourselves of her company. I suggested we go and look whether the station was guarded and luckily she said she wanted to rest her feet. The three of us then ambled away, and I alerted the Frenkels to the danger she represented. We decided it would be safer to leave her to her ice cream and departed. Fortunately she did, in the end, get to Switzerland.

As we had seen that the German military police was busy checking I.D. cards at Essen station, we decided to walk to the hamlet De Wildert, the next stop for the local train to Antwerp. It turned out that we were in for a good hike, but the marvellous weather and the delight at having successfully taken our first hurdle, made us close to jubilant. Inspired by the stretch of notorious Belgian cobblestones in front of us, it was not long before the three of us, to all appearances blissfully ignorant of any war at all, were stepping out smartly to a most forceful rendering of The Yellow Brick Road which clearly had to make up in enthusiasm what it lacked in musical quality. Who exactly was the Scarecrow-without-a-brain, the Tin-man-without-a-heart, and who the Lion-without-courage did not seem terribly important. Our spirited performance did, however, draw the attention of a couple of Belgian gendarmes who, wondering where we were going and why so happily, asked for our papers just to be sure. Mau and Siet produced their squeaky clean forged Belgian documents and I my perfectly legal

Dutch I.D. card which, fortunately, interested them much more! When they noticed that I was born in Bandung, "in the colonies", they suggested, tongue in cheek, that we must be on our way to the Congo (which was then still a Belgian colony and not in Nazi hands!). Clearly, these sterling chaps were not about to cause us any trouble, and happily accepted the story that I had met my "Belgian friends" by chance at the border and was just accompanying them part of the way to Brussels. To clinch the fact that we were totally above board, I asked them if I could leave my bicycle at their police station and pick it up again on my return.

This strategy worked perfectly, and we were waved on to continue our journey, once again singing loudly and celebrating the success of our first brush with officialdom. When we were out of earshot I urged the Frenkels to remember how one can often bluff one's way out of danger by being cool, calm and collected and using one's imagination.

As marching and singing on this sunny day made us thirsty, and the orchards along the road tempted us with their abundance of fruit, we were soon lying down on the shaded grass where we, unwisely, munched too many unripe apples. Suddenly we heard a loud rumbling, as of thunder in the distance, and the screech of German fighter planes screaming to the coast. It was, of course, August 19th, 1942 and what we heard was the thunder of the British raid on Dieppe!

As we found out later, this raid was also the reason why the Frenkels' *passeur* had not shown up at the border: he happened to live in Dieppe and most likely got killed. He was never heard of again! So, oddly enough, this whole story would probably not have been written if the British had carried out their raid on Dieppe at some later date!

All this had made the war real again and reminded me to give my inexperienced friends three "golden rules" for travelling through German occupied territory. First, don't sit together and do not speak to each other while on public transport; second, always make sure of an escape route wherever you are; and third, with appropriate modesty, never to forget that even the brightest German officer cannot hold a candle to the average Dutch student!

We then resumed our march and reached De Wildert without further incident. The Frenkels caught their train and I walked back to the Gendarmerie where I collected my bike, waved to the gendarmes, and cycled back across the border to Roosendaal along the same little country road. It vaguely occurred to me that this smuggling route might come in handy some day, although I did not have a clue of how, when and why.

ON THE SCENT

Back in Amsterdam I could report to the Frenkel parents, much to their relief, that I had seen their sons safely across the border.

Ten days later, however, father Frenkel suddenly contacted me to say that they had received a cryptic postcard which their sons had mailed in Brussels a day or so before. This clearly indicated that something unexpected must have happened to prevent them from continuing their journey. As Mathieu van den Berg was the only one who might know more about this, I promised the Frenkel parents that I would try and contact him via Lien van Beverwijk.

It was arranged that I would meet Mathieu, whose real surname was Smedts, at the home of Ward Messer, a journalist who had originally provided the contact in Roosendaal. They already knew that something had gone wrong but, as they were only in charge of the route up to the Belgian border, they had no idea of what could have happened.

When I told Ward and Mathieu about the smugglers road I had found, and how easy it had been to cross the border, they jumped at the prospects this offered. We decided that Mat and I should investigate further and at the same time try and find out what had happened to the Frenkels.

A few days later Mat and I bicycled down the smugglers road to Essen, and there took the train to Brussels. The *Feldgendarmerie* (German military police) did a random check of I.D. papers at Essen station and Mat was one of the very few who was not waved through. Routine caution meant that I was nowhere near him in the queue, so that I could make myself scarce in the event that Mat's forged Belgian papers would be spotted. Fortunately this did not happen, and a little while later we were recovering our composure in the train to Brussels. Mathieu told me that it was not the first time he had been singled out at an I.D. check. I wondered as to what would be so singular about him to attract attention so often. Could it be that his somber outlook on the world, which had arranged his features in an expression of permanent melancholy, made people think that he looked guilty and therefore must have something to hide? Anyway, we decided that it would be far safer to avoid official controls as much as possible.

My Brussels friends told us that the Frenkels had been in touch with a certain René Poupart, who lived on Avenue de Bois de Construction. So off we went. René turned out to be a nattily dressed and heavily scented slick, who was very suspicious at first but, after some to-ing and fro-ing, finally admitted that he had met the Frenkels and given them an address in Besançon. He could not, however, tell us whether they had actually got there.

We decided to find out. To get to Besançon we had to cross an administrative frontier of the German military command in northern France. Daan van der Putten told us that holders of a Belgian I.D. card could apply for a permit, for business trips only, at the Office de Compensation in Brussels.

Unhampered by any knowledge or experience we brazenly went there and asked for a permit to go on a wine buying trip to the Doubs region. In one of his books Mathieu Smedts described what happened next:

We had excellent Belgian papers, freshly forged and technically perfect. But we were so green, so terribly green!

Patiently we queued up at the counter of the Bank. Patiently we waited. And when someone called out our false names, I thought for a minute that we were already in France. But the little man behind the counter looked suspiciously German.

"Your papers are forged", he said – in German.

I protested.

"Do you want me to call Antwerp, where they have been issued? They are as alike as two peas in a pod. But never mind, I will help you."

I don't know why I did it, I had never bribed anybody before, but all of a sudden I found my hand passing a 1000 frank note across the counter.

"Come back in twenty minutes. I'll arrange everything. I'm from Luxembourg", he said. "The Gestapo is in the building".

We left. Henk strolled, I staggered, straight into the nearest café.

"Brandy", I ordered.

"We don't serve that", the waiter said.

"Don't be daft. We'll tip you well". How quickly one learns to live with corruption.

"Henk, we are not going back there!"

Now you are daft", Henk said. "Then we will have lost not only our papers, but also the fee of 3000 franks each, and the 1000 franks you used to grease that guy's palm!"

We went back. I was sweating.

We got our papers.

"Don't you also need French I.D. cards?" our little man asked, "I can get them". And he did, and not only for us, but also for countless Jews who, with his invaluable help, ended up safely in Switzerland!"

This enterprise not only provided us with superior forged Belgian and French papers and a useful contact with the Luxembourg Resistance but, above all, taught us the importance of maintaining one's *sang-froid* in a sudden crisis. Soon enough we were put to the test again.

At the administrative frontier in northern France the *Feldgendarmerie* was checking papers. The men had started at the back of the train and, with Teutonic thoroughness, were carefully scrutinising the documents of every single passenger.

With our experience in Essen still fresh in mind, I decided that it would not be very wise to sit and wait our turn. When the Germans got closer, we left the train through the door giving onto the tracks instead of the more usual one on the platform side which, as we could see, was guarded. We stealthily made our way to the back of the train and got on again in a carriage that had already been checked. The German policemen did not notice our manoeuvre and if any of the passengers did, they kindly chose to pretend otherwise.

We reached Besançon, and found the address which Poupart had given us: a little bistro across from the municipal abattoir, where we met a certain Raymond.

When we gave the password, he told us that, only two days ago, the Frenkels had been passed successfully across the demarcation line into unoccupied France and were safe from the Nazis. So, mission accomplished, we could return to Amsterdam and deliver the good news to the Frenkel parents.

IN THE FOOTSTEPS OF THE FRENKELS

The astounding ease with which we had been able to travel through German occupied territory, armed only with a stiff upper lip and some creativity, made us think that our knowledge and experience should be used to help other people escape from Nazi persecution.

Our little smugglers route between Roosendaal and Essen had proved to be quite safe. Its nerve centre was the Denissen farm, right on the Dutch-Belgian border, where we changed our Dutch and Belgian I.D. cards backwards and forwards. Things only got tricky once when, just after I had collected my Belgian I.D. card, I was stopped and checked by a German border guard who then wanted to know what I was doing on Dutch territory. Knowing that most Germans love a soppy story, I told him I was going to buy Dutch cheese for my poor mother who had a stomach condition and could only survive on a diet of Dutch cheese. Greatly impressed by my display of filial concern, he let me off with the warning that he did not ever want to see me there again. I walked off and joined Mat who had been watching the encounter from a safe distance, petrified and quite convinced that it would be the end of me!

Mathieu and I now got busy with the organisation of a safe escape route for Jews from Holland via our Brussels connections to Switzerland. Two more "minders" were recruited to bring refugees to Brussels: Dries Ekker, a journalist colleague of Ward Messer, and one of my friends from "Het Nieuwe Suyckerhofje", Dick van Stokkum, a medical student who, on his own, had also found a smugglers route to Belgium, near Putte.

It also occurred to me that our route could be used by couriers between the Resistance and the Dutch Government-in-Exile in London. I mentioned this at a Parool meeting with Jan Meijer and Wim van Norden at the safe house of Jaap Nunes Vaz in Wageningen. We decided that I should try and extend the route all the way to Switzerland, circumventing the money grabbing *passeurs* as much as possible. Jan Meijer gave me an address in Brussels, Rue Leonardo da Vinci, where I would find a man called Meesters whom he knew to be reliable and resourceful. Jan also gave me a set of detailed microfilmed maps of the German defences of the Dutch coast, which he wanted me to pass on to the British Secret Service in Switzerland. It just goes to show how green we were, that nobody realised that we could not expect to get access to the Secret Service without any corroboration.

So I went to Brussels where I got in touch with Meesters and introduced myself as a friend of Jan Meijer. He received me nicely

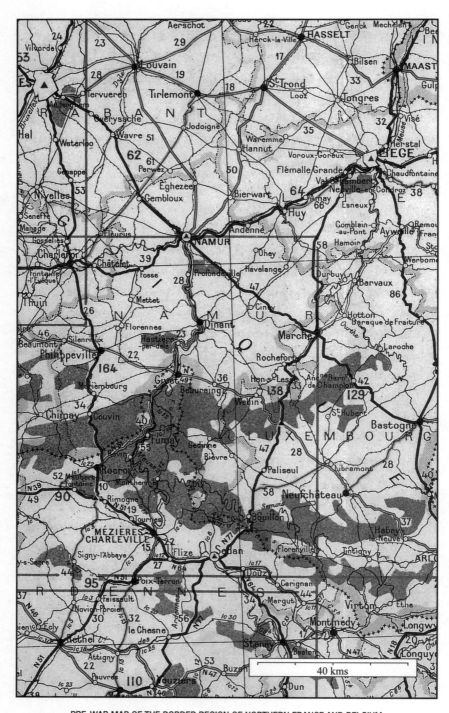

PRE-WAR MAP OF THE BORDER REGION OF NORTHERN FRANCE AND BELGIUM

enough but, when I told him about the microfilms, he became a bit too interested in my well-being and too eager to see the material. It made me suspicious and I thought it prudent to pretend not to have the films on me. I asked him if he knew a way to get me into Switzerland and he told me that he knew a *passeur*, a fine fellow, a professional acrobat who knew the Alsace-Swiss border like the back of his hand. Unfortunately, he was away and would not be back in Brussels for another two days, when I could come back to meet him.

On the appointed day I cautiously followed a common Resistance routine and arrived half an hour early for my meeting with the *passeur*. Only Meesters' girlfriend, Helena Lam, was there and she was so anxious that I should wait for her lover and his *passeur* that she flung all her not inconsiderable charms at me. But the lovely Helena's sudden interest in me only made me smell a rat and I decided that, maybe, I had better do without the acrobat. I told the lady that I was just going round the corner to get some cigarettes and bolted. I later found out that my suspicious mind had saved my life.

The train journey to Besançon was uneventful and upon arrival I went to the now familiar bistro and told Raymond that I wanted to get into unoccupied France. He then took me to the local *Chef de Résistance* who questioned me thoroughly on the purpose of my trip. He was only lukewarm about my plan to establish a courier route between Holland and Switzerland, but when I told him that I was carrying espionage material, he got very interested indeed. He gave me a French I.D. card in the name of a student from the Alsace (to account for my accent), who was born in Oran, Algeria, a useful place of birth as its records could not be checked in France. He also gave me the address of a Gaullist friend of his in Lyon, who owned a hotel where I would find a safe place to stay.

I was taken to a remote farm near the *ligne de démarcation*, the border between occupied and unoccupied France, where I had to hide in a barn under a pile of straw and wait for the *passeur*. I was there for a whole day. The *passeur* turned out to be a *passeuse*, a young girl by the name of Paulette who had also smuggled the Frenkels across.

At dusk the two of us took off, walking cross-country, using the cover of a small wooded slope which gave us a good view of the movements of the German patrols. We crossed over safely, and I made my way to Lyon. I found the Gaullist who apparently had already been informed about me and, upon hearing the password, received me like an old friend. This was a great relief, as I had felt curiously unsafe in a city without German uniforms but amidst civilians many of whom would not hesitate to hand me over to the local Gestapo.

My Gaullist friend, who knew that I was carrying espionage material, warned me that if the *Police Laval*, the security forces of the Vichy administration, would find this on me, they would probably shoot me on the spot. He knew a former French army officer who now worked for the British Secret Service and suggested that he contact him. This seemed sensible, and a meeting was set up.

The French officer was rather off-hand. He looked at the microfilms with some suspicion and asked me if I had a Secret Service codename or number. I had neither, of course, and explained that the microfilms had got into the hands of the Resistance after the agent who had produced them had been shot by the Germans. He looked doubtful, but nevertheless promised me to approach his British contact and find out whether they were interested. He did not want to hold on to the films, which made me feel confident that I was dealing with a professional. A few days later he sent word that the British were "not interested" because they had no idea who I was and had no interest in the Dutch coastal defences anyway! So, I resumed my trip to Switzerland, rather disappointed that I had not been able to get rid of my Damocles' sword.

As Paulette had told me that she had sent the Frenkels on to Annemasse I also went there. I arrived without further incident and decided at dawn to try and walk cross-country into Switzerland.

This looked easy enough, but after just a few hundred yards I was arrested by a Swiss border-guard. My French I.D. card was confiscated and they took me to a refugee centre at the Geneva stadium for further interrogation.

The place was crowded with refugees many of who told me, to my horror, that they had been there for months. I was much surprised therefore when I was transferred to the Chief Constable's office the very next day and put in a holding cell pending my interrogation. As I expected to be searched, I decided to get rid of the microfilms. Until then I had carried them in a matchbox with a double bottom, switching to a local brand whenever I moved into a different country. Now I hid the matchbox behind the radiator in my cell, and hoped fervently that I would be returned to the same cell after the interrogation.

The police commissioner who questioned me, clearly did not believe a word of my story that I had travelled all the way from Holland in pursuit of two Jewish friends of mine, just to be able to reassure their parents! He made me repeat my story three times over, shaking his head in disbelief. As he apparently could not make up his mind as to what to do with me, I was returned to my cell to await his decision. There I was horrified to find that the matchbox had disappeared. My cell had obviously been searched with Swiss precision. This meant big trouble! I was hardly surprised to be kept under lock and key that night.

I later found out that the microfilms, "authenticated" by having passed through Swiss hands, were sold for a bundle to the same British Secret Service that had refused them as a gift!

IN THE HANDS OF THE POLICE LAVAL

The next morning two policemen, without a word of explanation, came and escorted me to a van. It was an unpleasant surprise to hear from the people already in there that, at the Swiss-French border we would be handed over to the *Police Laval*. During the short trip the Swiss guards kept throwing me furtive glances and I was clearly the subject of their muttered conversation. Moreover, they treated me with great kindness, most unusual for Swiss policemen, and I got the distinct impression that they thought it most unfair that I was being sent back.

The Police Laval questioned me briefly and then I was taken by train straight to the *camp de résidence forcée* (internment camp) at Chateauneuf-les-Bains. There I found a motley crew of some sixty refugees, a few Dutchmen amongst them, mostly chaps who had escaped from the occupied territory or POW camps and had been apprehended en route to Switzerland or Spain.

I thought it odd that this camp did not seem to have the usual accoutrements of fence or barbed wire and I assumed it would be mere child's play to escape. But it took me only a day to find out the hard way what perfidious manacle was used to make sure that the inmates would stay put! The nearest railway station was closely guarded around the clock, and the next station, Riom, was 16 km away. The camp was a former spa, renowned for the benefit of its waters to patients suffering from persistent constipation.

The spa water, which was very rich in magnesium salts, was the only drinking water available. This meant that within 24 hours from arrival all prisoners were suffering from the runs and had to make a dash for it a dozen times a day! This unpleasant condition made it virtually impossible for anyone to abscond without leaving a malodorous trail, a doddle for even a French-trained dog to follow. But, as I had no intention wasting my time in a French spa, I decided that I had better apply some serious thought to solving this problem of chronic intestinal hyperactivity.

On arrival I had fortunately, truthfully for once, registered as a medical student and the very next day I was summoned to the office of the camp doctor. He was a Roumanian refugee who had "volunteered" to take on the medical care in the camp in exchange for a residence permit, but seemed far more interested in earning a bob or two from his private practice than in treating prisoners for free. My status as medical student obviously gave him the chance he had been waiting for, as he wanted to know how far along I was in my studies. When he was satisfied that I was familiar with first aid and the basic principles of pharmacology, he appointed me on the spot as his locum in charge of the infirmary and the dispensary. Naturally I jumped at this arrangement, as it gave me an unexpected opportunity to prepare my escape! I systematically started to skip the roll calls which were held three times a day in the courtyard, way below my infirmary window. They would call my name and get no response. And just when the camp management was getting really upset, I would pop my head out of the window of my eyrie and yell down cheerfully: *"à l'infirmerie!"*. Relieved sighs all round, and the roll call would gratefully roll on.

After a few days everybody was so used to this procedure that it was not even necessary for me to respond at all, as there was always someone who got fed up with the delay and would report me *"à l'infirmerie!"*. This was exactly what I needed to get a comfortable head start for my escape.

On Sunday the first roll call was at noon, so I figured that if I would abscond on Saturday afternoon, my absence would go undetected for at least 18 hours. I confided my plan to the cook, a nice chap from Rotterdam, and asked him to do the honours for me at evening roll call. He agreed, on condition that, in return, I would go and see his girlfriend in Rotterdam and tell her that he was all right and still very much in love with her.I promised to deliver this romantic message and he gratefully provided me with a loaf of bread and some salted fishes to sustain me on my trip. Now I only had to deal with the diarrhoea problem. This was not too difficult, however, as I had access to the dispensary where I had spotted a bottle of belladonna tincture, a big draught of which would curb the excessive bowel movements long enough not to leave a smelly trail and reach Riom undetected.

My plan worked like a dream. I walked through the night and reached the railway station at dawn. As I needed help and, especially, enough money to get back to Amsterdam, I had decided to try and get to my Gaullist friend in Lyon. When the Riom ticket office opened I found that I had only enough money to get to Roanne, and from there I would have to walk the N7 to Lyon.

It was the end of October 1942 and a glorious autumn day. The gently sloping hills of the Montagnes du Lyonnais with their glowing purple vines spotted with the deep blue of fully ripened grapes, curved up to the brilliant azure sky, in which the mauve veils of the coming night softened the last rays of the setting sun. The overwhelming beauty of this scenery made me forget my tiredness and also, almost, a broken sole which punctuated every other step with an annoying "flap".

I still had some small change in my pocket, just enough to pay for a train ticket for the last lap of my journey, from Tarare to Lyon. Once there I rushed to see my Gaullist friend. He gave me a large drink and listened to my story with a great many Gallic exclamations and eyes big with amazement. From that day onwards he referred to me as *"ce sacré flamand"* (that confounded Dutchman).

The next day, my first problem was to get some cash. I went to see "Fat Sally" Noach, the honorary Dutch consul in Lyon, who was known to be helpful without asking too many questions of stray Dutchmen turning up at his office. And helpful he was, even after I had told him that I planned to go back to Holland, whereupon he declared me completely "meshugge".

Back at the hotel of my Gaullist friend I found, much to my surprise, a Dutch journalist named Van Eck, whom I had met in the camp of Chateauneuf-les-Bains.

He told me that my escape had caused a tremendous stir amongst the guards, which had given him and a few other inmates the opportunity and impetus to follow in my footsteps. It was by chance that he knew of the same hotel. When I told him that I was going back to Holland and could get a *passeur* and forged French I.D. cards, he asked if he could join me and offered, in return, to cover our expenses. Our host then contacted the Resistance cell in Besancon, and soon got word that we should go to a farm near the *"ligne de démarcation"*, where we would be collected eventually.

At the farm we had to hide in the haystack for two days and obviously, in the end, we both looked less than perfectly groomed.

It was again Paulette who smuggled us safely across the border back into occupied France. She also gave us brand new French I.D. cards which only still needed to be signed by the departmental Prefect. She told us that we would get the signatures, forged of course, from the *Chef de Résistance* in Besançon. When we walked into the street where this man lived, however, we ran into a hitch, as one of the dreaded German police vans was parked in front of his house, and we could see the SD arresting the unfortunate at gunpoint in his own front room! So there went our precious route to Switzerland!

We managed to keep to a sedate walk to just around the corner, but then ran hot-foot to the railway station, where we took the first train to Nancy. First of all we had to forge the Prefect's signature on our I.D. cards. We managed to find an empty compartment, which was rather essential as we did not really want anybody watching us. For want of an authentic sample, we had to invent a signature. The risk of discovery seemed slight, considering that we would need these I.D. cards only up to Brussels. In any case, we had no choice. Little did we know how soon our forgeries would be put to the test!

No sooner had we committed to memory our new fictitious personal data, when, at the next station, a number of German soldiers boarded the train. On their way to the *Wehrmachtsabteilung* – carriages reserved for German army personnel which, for security reasons, were always located in the middle of the train – they had to pass our compartment. Much to our dismay, an elderly corporal, obviously rather the worse for wear, had the ungodly idea to enter our compartment, in spite of the loud protestations from his comrades that it was the wrong carriage. Without a word he sat down, took off his pack, got out a sausage and a lump of German bread, and proceeded to devour these before our ravenous eyes. We stoically looked out of the window with all the indifference our rumbling stomachs could muster.

When he had finished his meal with a last long draught from his hip-flask, he suddenly turned to us and asked, in thickly slurred German, who the devil we were. As our I.D. cards showed us to be from the Alsace, we could not reasonably pretend not to understand him. So we told him that we were students, that we had worked in the grape harvest and were now on our way home. Although this story should account both for our scruffy looks and our command of the German language, he kept watching us with obvious suspicion. Suddenly his befuddled brain seemed to have come to a conclusion, for he barked at us: *"Sie sind entwischte Kriegsgefangenen!"* (You are escaped POWs). Unimpressed by our vehement denial, he demanded to see our I.D. cards. Now the shit really hit the fan! No sooner had he noticed that we were from the Alsace or he jumped up in a sudden rage and started cursing at us. Apparently he had already been in the army during WWI and had never got over the German defeat. His pet hate was reserved for "those from the Alsace" who had so treasonably allowed themselves to be swallowed up by France and were therefore beneath contempt. As to our I.D. cards, "with scum like us they were bound to be fakes". We protested that in our heart of hearts we had always remained pro-German as was obvious from the fact that we still spoke German so well, but it was all to no avail. He stuffed our I.D. cards down his pocket and swore that he would personally hand us over to the *Feldgendarmerie* in Nancy.

We were obviously in deep trouble and our only hope was to negotiate our way out of this mess. So I started a friendly chat, telling him that we had been working at an uncle's farm when I got a message that my mother was gravely ill and to return home immediately. Surely he would understand that any delay might mean that I would not get home in time. If only he could show us why he thought that our documents were not genuine we were sure we could clear up this misunderstanding. I tried to impress on him that this would also be in his own interest as he surely would not want to make a fool out of himself at the *Feldgendarmerie*. Even in his befuddled state this seemed to make sense to him, as he took our I.D. cards from his pocket and tried to bring them into focus. I helpfully translated the French to him, told him a few jokes about French bureaucracy and distracted his attention enough to be able to, surreptitiously, put our documents back into my own pocket.

We desperately kept up this small talk with our drunken soldier, whom we now knew as Karl, and hoped to make him forget the unappealing idea to have us arrested in Nancy. It seemed to work for a while, until we inadvertently put our foot in it again. He once more demanded our papers and we were back at square one!

Meanwhile I had found out that Karl was actually on leave and on his way to the fleshpots of Paris. He asked me if I had ever been there. With a wink, I quickly assured him that I had intimate knowledge of the place and soon had him licking his chops at my description of a lively parade of Parisian mam'selles whose, totally fictitious, names, addresses and specialities he painstakingly jotted down in his notebook. This absorbing occupation meant that he failed to notice the sleight of hand by which I managed to move both I.D. cards safely back to my own pocket again.

When our train pulled into Nancy station, Karl was still busy scribbling his notes, tongue between his teeth. I hastily took my leave, wished him a great time in Paris, and was already in the corridor when he called: "*Warte mal, wir müssen noch zur Feldgendarmerie!*" (Hang on, we still have to go to the MP's). I noticed that Van Eck could not get through while Karl was still clumsily putting on his kit. I shouted "*Aber mach schnell, Mensch*" (hurry up, man), "you will miss the train to Paris" and continued to move to the exit. He stumbled behind me but, with his vision diminished not only due to the blackout but also to his alcoholic haze, he did not notice that the door that I so politely held open for him gave onto the tracks instead of onto the platform. The resounding crash with which he landed was most satisfactory and, having gently closed the door on the stream of obscenities emanating from the dark, I quickly joined the crowd on the platform looking for Van Eck. I had to find him as I had both I.D. cards, but he had all the money, so neither of us could get to Brussels alone.

It is not easy to find somebody on a crowded, blacked-out station. But, as the train to Brussels was not due to leave for an hour, I had lots of time. When most people had gone however, and there was still no trace of Van Eck, I assumed he had thought it safer to wait for me outside the station. So I went to look for him on the pitch-black station square, where I tried to catch his attention by whistling the "Wilhelmus" (the Dutch national anthem), but to no avail. Had he been arrested after all? But then he would not be able to produce his I.D. card, which in itself was a serious offence and was bound to lead to even more trouble!

The only way to find out was from the police, which meant going to the dreaded *Feldgendarmerie* after all. If Van Eck had indeed been arrested, the only chance he had was if I turned up and tried to talk him out of trouble.

With some trepidation I went to beard the lion in his den and found, to my shock, that the officer-in-charge was an *SS-Oberscharführer* (sergeant) and not one of the regular MP's. I thought I would try to play on the well-known acrimony between the SS and the Wehrmacht.I snapped to attention and addressed the sergeant as *Herr Sturmscharführer* (warrant officer), which produced a Cheshire Cat smile. I told him that my friend and I had met a Gefreiter (army corporal) on the train, who had wanted to arrest us as he thought our I.D. cards were not in order, but that I had lost both the soldier and my friend in the crowd, and now wanted to find out please if Herr Sturmscharführer perhaps was holding my friend in custody?

Taking the bait hook, line and sinker, the SS-man started raging at the *verdammte Unverschämtheit* (damned impertinence) of a *Wehrmachtsangehöriger* (member of the regular army) who had the bloody cheek to disregard all regulations and meddle with the authority which was the exclusive province of the SS! I was overjoyed at the obvious success of my ploy and wasted no opportunity to fan the rage of the affronted bureaucrat. Eventually he showed me the list of the prisoners who had been brought in that day but, to my relief, neither the real Van Eck nor his alias was on it. With much clicking of heels, I thanked *Herr Sturmscharführer* for his *ausserordentlich bereitwillige Hilfeleistung* (exceptionally courteous help and assistance) and saluted him with a fervent *"Heil Hitler"*. He crisply sprang to attention and advised me to go to the French *Chef de Gare* (stationmaster) and ask him to broadcast my friend's name over the public address system. I thanked the *Scharführer* again for this very valuable piece of advice, but chuckled inwardly at the thought of Van Eck's horror at hearing such a broadcast, no doubt the surest way to make him vanish into the woodwork for good.

For want of a better plan, I decided to board the always overcrowded and blacked-out train to Brussels and take my chances at reaching my destination without a ticket.

We left and, as luck would have it, some Customs Officers came round to check for contraband. As they were using a torch, I asked them if I could come with them to look for my lost friend who had to be somewhere on the train. This was no problem and I duly found Van Eck dozing in a corner a few carriages along. He was delighted to see me and had, to my relief, bought me a ticket, which I happily swapped for his I.D. card.

We reached Brussels the next morning without further incident, and said goodbye. It was November 4th, 1942. I never saw Van Eck or heard of him again.

MATHIEU GETS CAUGHT

Upon arrival I went directly to the Van der Puttens in the Rue Jules le Jeune, where I had the loveliest bath of my life, a refreshing shave and a delicious breakfast, the likes of which I had not seen for many weeks.

Feeling human again, I next went to the Rue Jeanne, our safe house for Jewish refugees on their way to Switzerland. There I found Dries Ekker, busily organising the transport of about eight refugees. He told me that, any moment, he was expecting Mathieu to arrive who, together with two others, Binnert de Beaufort and Anja Horowitz, urgently had to go to Switzerland as the Gestapo was hot on their trail in Holland. When I told them how our Besançon route had been blown by the SD their faces fell. This was, of course, a serious setback and one for which we had no ready solution.

I then went to the Rue Leonardo da Vinci, to tell Meesters that I had managed to find a route to Switzerland, but that part of it could not be used at present. As soon as I walked in, Meesters demanded to know what had happened to the microfilms. When I told him that I had lost them in Switzerland, he yelled at me and told me off for not having waited for the *passeur* whom he had arranged especially for me. When I had calmed him down a bit, he also told me that Jan Meijer and Wim van Norden had been arrested, that the Gestapo was after me too and that I should, under no circumstances, return to Holland. He would find me a safe house in Belgium where I could lie low for a while.

I said that I would think about it and also wanted to discuss it with my friends. I told him of the trouble they were in because of the collapse of our escape route to Switzerland. Then Meesters (who really was a Nazi agent, called Van Poppel, as we found out after the war!) came up with a "brilliant" idea. He told me that he was just putting together an escape route to Portugal, and suggested that my friends could use that. If they were interested, I was to bring them round that night.

As Mathieu's little party wanted to find out more about this Portuguese route, the four of us did indeed go to Meesters' place in the Rue Leonardo da Vinci that evening. There we were introduced to a certain Doctor Bodens, a supposed GP from Limburg, who spoke Dutch with a distinct German accent. According to Meesters this man was high up in the Resistance and would be prepared to get me a safe house and the necessary food coupons.

The discussion about the Portugese arrangements turned out to be highly frustrating as Meesters kept going round and round in circles without ever coming to the point. Mathieu describes the events of that evening:

The discussion was going nowhere. Our host had a very well stocked drinks cabinet, a trifle suspicious at the end of 1942. Although my friends and I managed to stay sober, he himself partook with gusto. He had also invited a SOI-DISANT doctor, who was introduced to us as one of the top people in the Belgian resistance (........) The booze, Van Poppel's girlfriend and his verbal diarrhoea gave me the creeps. I did not actually distrust him yet, but he mentioned so many names that it made me feel uncomfortable Our golden rule was never to gossip. And this man was a real chatterbox. (.......) After a while Binnert de Beaufort whispered to me: "Why are you so quiet?" "We should have a serious chat before we agree to go with him", I said. "He talks too much. If he is ever caught, we have also had it." (.........)

It was already late when the doctor offered to drive us home. I asked him to drop us somewhere near our safe house I did not want these loose tongues to know the exact address.

Henk Pelser was sitting next to the driver. Binnert de Beaufort, the Jewish girl and I were in the back. Nobody was talking, because of the tension which had developed during the evening. Suddenly the car stopped. "There is a mailbox just around the corner", the doctor said. "Would you mind posting this letter for me?" Henk got out. Suddenly all hell broke loose. We heard hoarse shouting. A searchlight was aimed at us. The doors of the car were jerked open.

"Hands up!"

"Henk has escaped", Binnert whispered.

"Schnabel halten," (shut up) a German yelled. In a few short seconds disaster was upon us.

What Mathieu did not know was that the doctor had already asked me before if I knew the Rue des Deux Eglises, as he had to deliver a letter there. I remembered having seen it on my way to Meesters' house, running off the Rue de la Loi and offered to show him the way. This is why I sat in front. When we got close to the street, I told the doctor to slow down and, before he knew what I was doing, had jumped out of the car to look if it was indeed the right street. All of a sudden I was caught in the blinding glare of a searchlight mounted on a car behind us. To be able to see what was happening, I stepped out of the lightbeam and saw several armed men pouring out of the car, shouting: *"Hände hoch!"* (hands up). It was pretty obvious that they were bad news!

As I had moved out of the light so quickly, they had never spotted me, and I was able to take cover in a doorway and watch from there. All the occupants of the doctor's car were arrested, and pretty soon both cars drove off.

I rushed to the nearest phonebox to alert Meesters to what had happened and tell him to make a run for it but, to my dismay, some German answered the phone. I assumed that Meesters had been arrested too, and hung up without a word. I now had to tell Dries and, as fast as my legs could carry me, I ran to the Rue Jeanne, where I managed to arrive just before the curfew. We spent the rest of the night destroying incriminating documents and waited for the curfew to be lifted when we could start evacuating the refugees and a hot potato called Dekker who was high on the hit list of the *Abwehr* (German counterintelligence service) and whom we had in hiding until he could be moved to England.

Only after the war did we learn that Dekker was actually an agent of the Dutch Section of the British SOE (Special Operations Executive) whose real name was George Dessing. He had been airdropped into Holland with instructions to get Koos Vorrink to England. But Vorrink refused to go and Dessing could not get in touch with the SOE as not only had his radio operator been killed but all other SOE agents had been caught and were being used by the *Abwehr* as stoolpigeons in their notorious *"Englandspiel"*. Dessing narrowly escaped arrest himself and by chance got in touch with Dick van Stokkum and Jet Roosenburg who brought him to our place in Brussels. He had then contacted the Belgian Resistance who had promised him to warn the SOE about the games the *Abwehr* was playing in Holland. Unfortunately, for unknown reasons, this message never got through. Dessing only got back to England in September 1943.

Dries and I were counting on Mathieu and the other two to be able to hold up under German interrogation long enough to enable us and the refugees to get away safely. They did not fail us, and everybody, Dekker and the tenants of the house included, got out as soon as the curfew had been lifted. None of the refugees, bar one, ever realised the danger they had been in.

Through the morning twilight we shepherded our little flock to the railway station and handed them over to the usual *passeur*. They all got to Switzerland safely. We found out later that the SD had been at the door of the safe house less than an hour after we had left it!

ARRESTS AT *HET PAROOL*

As Meesters had told us that the Germans were after me, we agreed that it was safer if I stayed in Brussels while Dries for whom, as far as we knew, they were not looking, went to Amsterdam to check out the situation there.

I had a safe address at Margot Nyst's. I knew her through her sister,

Lison Muntz, who lived in Amsterdam and was a friend of Hans Warendorf. I had, in the past, smuggled her into Brussels a few times for her to visit her parents. Dries in the meantime, rushed to warn Ward Messer and Dick van Stokkum that Mathieu had been arrested and that the safe house in the Rue Jeanne could no longer be used. Moreover, we were desperate to know if Jan Meijer and Wim van Norden had indeed been arrested, and what the implications were for our own security. Dries found out that Wim van Norden had been taken first and Jan Meijer and Jaap Nunes Vaz shortly afterwards on October 27th and 28th respectively, but that nobody knew what had happened to Hans Warendorf.

Two days later Dries was back in Brussels. We decided to check out the situation at the Rue Jeanne. With our key we entered the house through the basement door and discovered that upstairs the lights were on, whereupon we beat a silent, if hasty, retreat. We then telephoned and somebody answered who pretended to be the tenant. When we suggested that we meet in a nearby cafe, this person agreed just a little too eagerly. To our trick question: "How do we recognise each other?", he suggested that we should wear a buttonhole. As the impostor obviously did not know that the man he pretended to be knew both of us very well, he unwittingly gave himself away as a Gestapo agent. Needless to say we did not bother to keep the appointment.

As, in spite of the Parool arrests, there appeared to be no immediate danger to us, we decided to go back to Amsterdam as somebody had to find out what had happened to Hans Warendorf. I went to see his wife, who told me in tears, that Hans had suddenly disappeared on October 29th. She suspected that he might have gone to Paris, where he had a friend, Van Nierop, whose address she gave me. When, later, I saw Hans in Paris, he told me that it had taken him 10 days to get there via Maastricht and Brussels where, in retrospect perhaps fortuitously, he missed me by just one day.

We found out after the war that the arrest of Jan Meijer, Wim van

Norden and Jaap Nunes Vaz had occurred because Meesters, alias Van Poppel, who was an *Abwehr* agent with special instructions to infiltrate into the Resistance, had reported that they were involved in the smuggling of sensitive intelligence (no doubt my microfilms!) to the Allies. What the Germans did not know, however, was that these three, together with Hans Warendorf and Cees de Groot, were the editors of the *Hetzschrift* (subversive pamphlet) *Het Parool*.

With Hans Warendorf in Paris, Cees de Groot was the only editor left, which meant that the very survival of the paper was at stake. This was serious enough in itself in view of the importance of *Het Parool* to the Resistance but, even more, because a sudden discontinuation of the publication would signal to the Gestapo that the badly wanted but maddeningly elusive editors of *Het Parool* must have been caught. This would, of course, seriously endanger Jan Meijer and the others in custody.

As Cees de Groot had gone into hiding and, for obvious reasons, was not keen on a meeting with me as I had the shadow of the Gestapo hanging over me, the only one left of the Parool group known to me who had not been arrested, was Jan Stallinga. Jan put me in touch with Gerrit-Jan van Heuven Goedhart, an experienced journalist who had joined the Resistance and had previously contributed columns to *Het Parool*. We had a long talk in which he told me that he had had a meeting with Cees, and had agreed to be acting Editor-in-Chief of *Het Parool*. He said that it would be very useful to him if I could try and locate Hans Warendorf to get some editorial policy suggestions from him.

So, although we were on the Gestapo's "Wanted" list, we now had two urgent reasons to carry on: we had to locate Hans Warendorf and we still had to find a usable route to Switzerland. We set to work immediately.

IV

THE SCOUTS

LOOKING FOR A TRAIL OF OUR OWN

Because the *passeurs* were unnerved by the Brussels *Gestapo's* dramatic arrest of our friends, their prices became usurious. By the end of November 1942 the passage from Brussels to Switzerland cost roughly 9,000 guilders per head – the price of a middle class house in pre-war Amsterdam. We must give them credit however: they always kept their part of the bargain and all the refugees we put in their care reached their destination safely. But their prices became more and more prohibitive. Initially we had overcharged wealthy refugees to pay for the escape of some less well off people. This was becoming impossible. Therefore we had to look for a way to circumvent our Brussels intermediaries.

Our wonderful friend Margot Nyst had contacts with the *Witte Brigade* (White Brigade), a Belgian Resistance organisation, through which she could supply us with excellent Belgian and French I.D. cards on 24 hours notice. This made us independent of our former suppliers.

The next step was to see René Poupart, the man who had all the details of the *passeurs'* route to Switzerland. This time, René was not quite so hospitable. I told him that the *Gestapo* was hot on our heels and that Dries and I needed his route, as we had to leave for Switzerland immediately. Although his every business instinct rebelled at the thought of sharing his lucrative knowledge with me, he nevertheless realised that he would never get rid of my dangerous presence unless he gave me the information I wanted. Eventually he stopped prevaricating and gave me the complete route to Switzerland, including the names of the *passeurs* and the passwords. In return, I promised him that, in my stead, Dick van Stokkum would continue the activities that provided Poupart with such a generous income. However, just to be on the safe side, Dries and I decided to check the route to make sure that Poupart had not double-crossed us.

On December 2nd, 1942, we set off. Poupart's route led us by train to Bouillon. From there we were to take a taxi to Sedan. This turned out to be quite an experience. The driver of the taxi was a priceless character known as *"frère Jacques"* who obviously lived with a complete disdain for the concept of mortality. In the superannuated remains of what had once been a motorcar he tore along the potholed backcountry roads with death-defying panache and never a thought for his passengers who were sitting, petrified, on the back seat. We crossed the border at a spot which the German military command did not care about as it was not on an administrative frontier, and which had been left in the care of Belgian and French Customs Officers who guarded it with convenient *laissez-faire*.

In Sedan frère Jacques took us straight to his favourite watering hole as he knew that a stiff brandy was the only remedy for the mental disorder in which his passengers usually arrived. When we had sufficiently recovered, we took the train to Belfort, where we were supposed to locate an escaped Belgian convict called Paul Ruys.

On train journeys through France, Dries and I usually got stuck into some juicy French novel in order to avoid any conversation lest our accents should give us away as foreigners. We were reading, as usual, when the train, a little while before Belfort, had just passed the station of Lure and a passenger who had been dozing suddenly woke and asked Dries: *"C'était Lure ici?"* (have we passed Lure). Dries, looking up from his book, replied: *"Oui, Lure"*.At any other time Dries' less than perfect French accent would not be spotted in only two words. This time it had the most unforeseen consequences.

The next time I looked up from my book I noticed that another passenger had left our compartment and was now standing in the corridor from where he was staring at me most fixedly. When he had caught my eye, he beckoned me with an almost imperceptible movement of his head. As it seemed prudent to ignore him, I went back to my book. A few minutes later I looked up again and this time there was no mistaking the discreet summons. I decided to find out what he wanted and left my seat, ostensibly to stretch my legs. In the corridor I positioned myself in front of the window and produced a packet of Gauloises. I made a bit of a show of trying to find my matches to give the mystery man the opportunity to offer me a light, which he promptly did.

He struck up a rather odd conversation about the scenery that was rolling by and told me with rapture how much he loved the distant mountains where the air was so enticingly pure and from where one had such a stunning view of the land beyond which he called, with some emphasis, *"le pays de la liberté"*. "How many people", he sighed, "would not give a fortune to be able to get there!". "And you", he went on a bit too casually, "should surely understand that, as I can tell that you come from a country that has no mountains". I then knew that he had to be Belgian, as no Frenchman would be able to tell a Flemish from a Dutch accent in French. And when he hinted that he could show me a lovely road through the foothills it suddenly struck me that he was touting for business for a *passeur*, either himself or a third party. He probably took me for a *passeur* working the Belgian-French border!

The combination Belgian-*passeur*-Belfort made the penny drop and I stopped him in his tracks by stating calmly: *"Et vous êtes Paul Ruys!"*. He turned ashen, which was all the proof I needed! Before he could take to his heels I quickly whispered *"Outsiplou"* (see note 2), the curious password that Poupart had given us. Paul Ruys started breathing again and henceforth lived in the unshakable belief that Dries and I were redoubtable and dangerously professional underground agents.

I introduced Dries to our new best friend and we soon discovered how fortuitous this chance meeting had been. Paul Ruys told us that the Germans had posted an expert in French dialects at the exit of Belfort station, who could pick out a foreigner by the way he said *"Bonjour"*. However, he knew a way around this trap and he got us out of the station through a side door with the help of his buddy, the stationmaster.

Paul Ruys took us home where he poured some large brandies to recover his composure and toast our new friendship. We had a long chat and he turned out to be exactly the kind of man we were looking for. He did not need any prior notice as he had a number of very reliable *passeurs* to Porrentruy, Switzerland, on call and therefore was able to arrange for people to get across the border quickly for a fee of around 900 guilders per person. This was considerably less than Poupart had charged us!

A PARIS FLING

Having concluded our business with Paul Ruys, we now had to get to Paris and find Hans Warendorf. We mentioned that we were planning to travel back to Brussels along our by now well-trodden path and then try and find a route to Paris either via Lille or by heading due south. When Ruys heard this, he declared us stark staring mad but that same afternoon, December 5th, 1942, he put us on the direct Belfort-Paris train with strict instructions to the savvy conductor to help us across the tricky Somme-Aisne-Marne line, the border between the administrative districts of the German commands of Belgium and France respectively. The conductor was as good as his word and we got to Paris safely.

The train was riddled with black-marketeers and, while Dries had gone for a pee, I was offered some *"saucissons bien gras"* (good fat cold sausage), which I turned down as I was sure I would be short-changed. When I told Dries, he tore a strip off me and, as it turned out later, quite rightly so.

Our search for Hans Warendorf's address somewhere in the depths of Neuilly posed more of a problem than we had reckoned with. The address we had, turned out to be that of an office which had already closed when we got there. All we were able to find out was that we could not contact Hans till the following afternoon. This meant that the start of the curfew saw us lost in a dark, friendless and worse, hotelless, Paris suburb. We had no choice but to hide in the dark recesses of the first available basement well. A miserable place to spend the night at any time, but especially gruesome for two cold and hungry Dutchmen on St. Nicholas eve when tradition demands warmth, grog, sweets and lots of presents in the bosom of one's family.

Our rumbling stomachs kept us from sleeping (and Dries did not leave off reminding me as to exactly whose fault that was!) and we did not even dare light a cigarette for fear of the German patrols which, in fact, at one time came dangerously close to discovering us in the beam of their torches.

At the end of the curfew at 4 a.m. we made for the tempting warmth of the nearest Metro and spent the next few hours sleeping in turns while criss-crossing Paris for the price of a single ticket, always changing trains before the end-of-line station.

When Paris was finally beginning to wake up – which we had been checking for every time the train emerged from the tunnel and ran above ground – we headed for breakfast. As we had no ration cards, we were delighted to discover that we could get fed by the simple expedient of ordering coffee and brandy, when a croissant would be thrown in for free! The plan for the day was to see Hans Warendorf but also to do some frivolous shopping for our girlfriends in Amsterdam. Mine never stopped berating me for bringing her a lipstick, two Made in Paris silk scarfs and some Chanel No.5 scent, none of which she could wear in Holland without raising dangerous questions as to their provenance!

As we could not see Warendorf till later that afternoon, and our hungry night was an experience we did not care to repeat, we decided that a good French lunch was definitely in order. On our trips, money was one of the few things that was never a problem. We chose a pleasantly appointed restaurant and ordered a sumptuous lunch but ran into the bread-rationing problem again. Dries' sacrilegious suggestion that we could dine quite well without bread was met with such a display of Gallic outrage that it drew the most unwelcome attention of some German officers sitting in our vicinity. Dries efficiently silenced the voluble waiter with a note large enough to produce all the black-market bread that French culinary tradition demanded.

In excellent spirits after our delicious meal, we finally had our meeting with Hans Warendorf who was very happy to see me again and get to know Dries.

I discussed the Parool business with him and told him of our plan to use the Swiss route not only to transport refugees but also for information. Hans then suggested that, through Van Heuven Goedhart, we contact the last "Lord Lieutenant" of Utrecht, Jonkheer (note 3), L.H.N. Bosch Ridder van Rosenthal, an extremely well-connected man whose brother was the Dutch Ambassador in Switzerland.

THE ARREST OF THE MESSERS

We arrived back in Amsterdam two days later, where we were delighted to hear that Mathieu had managed to escape while en route from Brussels to a prison in Holland. We were also told that we had become No.1 on the Abwehr's "Wanted" list and that, for the past fortnight, all our known lairs had been searched and watched. But the hounds had been called off mere hours before we arrived, probably because by then they assumed that we had been warned.

The bad news was that Ward and Juta Messer had been caught by the Germans. How this happened we heard from Ward after the war:

It was Friday night, the November 27th, 1942. At about 9 p.m., the doorbell rang at Stadionkade 14 in Amsterdam, the address of our small ground floor flat. I pushed the button to open the main entrance and was just unlatching the door to our flat, when it and I were thrust back into the narrow hallway by four men. One of them pushed a gun into my side and yelled: "Hands up!" while the others, uniformed Germans, crowded around me. They flung open the door to the kitchen which was separated from the drawing room by a leaded window. I, meanwhile, had pushed the gun away from me and said, as soon as my heartbeat had returned: "This won't be necessary!". An elderly German motioned to the mackintoshed Dutchman to put the gun away and asked, as he could see Juta talking to another woman in the drawing room: "Wer ist diese Frau?" (who is that woman). "Eine Freundin meiner Frau" (a friend of my wife) I said. It was Wim Hora Adema, a co-editor of mine at the "Algemeen Handelsblad" (a well-known Dutch newspaper) who, like Dries Ekker and I, had quit the paper when it was taken over by pro-Nazis. There she was, long after curfew, sitting comfortably next to her old shopping bag with its camouflage of knitting sticking out but actually full of ration cards which she brought to us and other people who then distributed them onwards to Jews in hiding. Ever since Mathieu Smedts had moved in with us, these kinds of underground jobs had steadily grown in number: eventually we became a focal point. Apparently neither of the women had noticed what was going on in the little hallway. Then, suddenly, the five of us burst into the room. The Dutchman in the raincoat asked Wim Hora Adema who she was and when she said: "A friend", he told her to leave immediately. Neither she nor her bag were searched! "What a lucky devil", I thought "at least she will spread the word that we have been raided!" And she had indeed leapt into action immediately. She had stayed with us rather longer than she had meant. There was so much to talk about. She was there when, five minutes before curfew, Mr. and Mrs. Hirsch had knocked on our door and asked if they could spend the night in the spare room we had on the attic floor. They had been warned of a razzia that night in the South of Amsterdam. They were a young Jewish couple. He was a German emigré and his wife a designer at my mother-in-law's factory. They lived just around the corner in Rubensstraat, a few houses away from the notorious SS-Hauptsturmführer Aus der Fünten, who was in charge of the deportation of the Jews in Holland. Of course they could stay. We gave them the key and they went upstairs.

The spare room was available since Mathieu Smedts had left for Switzerland with a few companions and a lot of sensitive material. We had since heard, on the grapevine, that he had been arrested in Brussels. Early in the afternoon I had heard from a mutual acquaintance that one of our friends, Wim Ouweleen, had also been arrested that very morning. When I told Juta we both felt that the danger seemed to be closing in on us. I had put all forged I.D. cards and anything else incriminating in an old school bag which I then hid in a broom closet in the marble main entrance hall of our mansion block. Nobody could tell that this closet went with our flat. So our house was "clean" except for the ration cards which Wim Hora Adema had just brought us. I had hidden them under the dust jacket of a book, "Fairy Tales" by Godfried Bomans, which I had picked at random from the shelf and had returned to the row of books on top of our large mahogany bookcase that stood against the partition wall between our bedroom and the cubicle where our one year old first-born, Toontje, was asleep.

Meanwhile, the three Germans but especially the raincoated traitor had turned our tiny flat upside down in a vain search for the absent Smedts. No one thought to look in the attic! The Raincoat then started surveying the books, muttering that each and everyone of those would have to be scrutinised. Suddenly he yanked a book out of the row. I was flabbergasted when I saw that it was Bomans' "Fairy Tales" from which, in triumph, he shook the ration cards onto the ground. "I am Malowitz!!" he shouted, alluding to a magician who was a sensation in Amsterdam at the time. I noted with satisfaction that the Germans exchanged a look of contempt. The professional police detectives of the Abwehr, whose main job was the investigation of enemy agents, coded messages, tracing air-drops of radios or weapons and other counter-intelligence activities, looked down with great disdain on the SD and its use of traitors and informants in its purely political work of ferreting out resistance workers and the persecution of Jews.

(How did Raincoat "Malowitz" manage to pick out the exact right book from the shelve?! That question always puzzled me until, many years after the war, I asked a former detective who had also been active in the Resistance. "That's easy", he told me, "your bookcase had obviously not been dusted; that way a book that has been moved stands out like a sore thumb".)

"Malowitz" now talked non stop. He stirred the untidy pile of papers on my desk, barked that all would be confiscated, ordered me to unlock a small cubbyhole and triumphantly grabbed the banknotes that were in a steel moneybox inside. It was quite a bundle: about 4000 guilders, a considerable sum of money at the time. Most of it had been left with us by my mother-in-law when she was taken to Switzerland by Mathieu, and was to pay off a mortgage, and to serve as an emergency fund for Juta and me. The bastard took the lot!

In the meantime, Juta reappeared from the bedroom where one of the Germans had been interrogating her. She was terribly nervous and white with fear. Terrified she yelled at me, over the heads of the three Germans: "You know that I know nothing! You tell them!" She then asked to go to the loo. A little later I heard the flush and a scuffle. She had been made to leave the door half open and the German who had been guarding her came in with an I.D. card in his hand, shouting: "Das hat die Frau versucht hindurch zuziehen" *(She tried to flush this down)* and gave the card to his boss. Juta followed him into the room. She was in tears, mortified by the open loo door and panicked because of her failure to get rid of the I.D. card – one without a "J" that Dries and I had stolen for her at the Handelsblad office and which a forger friend had adapted for her.

While we had a moment of silent contemplation of the consequences of these latest developments, we suddenly heard the shrill sound of the doorbell ringing in the flat above. On his toes the Raincoat crept to the front-door of the flat and pushed the button to release the main entrance door. When he could *hear somebody come in, he threw the door to our flat wide open and barked: "Whom do you want?" I heard somebody answer with a confused stammer that he wanted the people upstairs. "No, you do not", said the Raincoat, "you want the Messers" and pulled a young man into the flat by his sleeve. I was in a chair, in handcuffs, and stared with spellbound fascination. I saw a rather tall young man, I would guess about eighteen years old, dressed in a kind of navy duffel coat with brass buttons, and totally bewildered. So, for that matter, was I; I did not know him from Adam!*

Raincoat quickly searched the lad's pockets but all he found was a small, folded piece of paper. They all inspected it. A diagram for a wireless! "Ha, it is the radio operator!" they cried. Did not every self-respecting spy ring need a radio operator? Well, here he was! The boy was shoved into the bedroom to be interrogated.

I was totally at sea. Who, for Pete's sake, was this guy? Had he really been going to see the ladies upstairs? In any case when, a little later, they took him away in handcuffs and he saw me, also in cuffs, still sitting in my drawing room chair, he angrily called out: "I have never laid eyes on that spy before!" Raincoat was sent off with the sailor. After all, it was his big catch!

The solution to the mystery was that the young man was actually a navy cadet, a lodger in the house of Wim Hora Adema's parents, who had been dispatched by Wim to warn the Hirsches in our attic of the danger downstairs. It turned out that they slept through the whole shenanigans and left peacefully the next morning, dropping the key in our letterbox.

The boy, whom they never managed to connect to us, spent about three months in jail and was then released. The supposed diagram for a transmitter turned out to be a design for the most basic crystal receiver!

Remarkably, the three Germans left in the flat now deliberated, at great length, on what should be done about the baby who was still fast asleep. Around the corner to the grandparents seemed the best bet. A little later our one-year-old, now wide awake, was wheeled into the drawing room by Juta and her armed guard. I was ordered to say good-bye. When I looked into the pram, the senior German, who had been observing me closely, muttered angrily to the others: "Da sieht man, das ist ein Härter!" *(Look what a hard nut this is!)* Mathieu Smedts later told me that the man's own son was drowned as a toddler and he was probably thinking that, if someone was saying good-bye to his son forever, he had to be very hard boiled to be so unemotional.

The door of the flat closed behind Juta, two months pregnant with our second child, and Toontje – the two of them closely guarded by two German soldiers, both armed to the teeth.

The senior German, SS-Sturmscharführer Bauer, was left behind in charge of me. He installed himself comfortably and started his interrogation. His very first question made clear that he worked for the Abwehr: "I want you to tell me everything you know about Smedts". "I will not say a word" I replied obstinately. He looked surprised. Like that, is it? "Why not?" he asked. "First we have to settle the business of my wife's I.D. card". I knew that mixed marriage Jews were also sent straight to the concentration camp for even a minor offence. "Why?" asked Bauer. "Because I know what Jews can expect in a place like Mauthausen" I retorted furiously. "Na, Mauthausen!" He muttered as though to say "why think the worst straightaway?". But I insisted and said that I refused to make any statement until the I.D. card had been destroyed and I had his word of honour that my wife would be released. Bauer sat and pondered, fingering the I.D. card. He then grabbed my sleeve and pulled me, cuffs and all, into the kitchen. He held the I.D. card over the sink, pulled out his lighter and let the document go up in flames. Juta's picture was the last bit to twist and blacken. Bauer opened the tap and the ashes were washed away.

Sturmscharführer Bauer probably got less out of our deal than he had hoped as, in my statements, I stuck to the scenario pre-arranged for events like this, which was to keep your mouth shut for at least 24 hours to give your mates a chance to cover their tracks and take on new identities. It was figured that the Gestapo would not get too rough within that time. In any case, Bauer obviously soon became persuaded that I had nothing to do with the spies he was after.

In spite of Bauer's promise, Juta spent almost seven weeks in a cell at the Amstelveenseweg jail. A transport of Jewish prisoners was deported from there every Thursday. The terror of being put on transport, the smell of mouldy straw *pallets and the lack of fresh air in a cell of six by twelve feet with six people inside, made her asthma so bad that she spent most of her time standing on a chair in front of the air vent. Eventually, she managed to be admitted to the sick-bay when she put a pillow under her skirt and pretended to be six months pregnant.*

Due to the Christmas holidays I was not interrogated again by Bauer until January 7th, 1943. In the meantime I had heard, even in prison, that Juta was still in custody. I bitterly berated Bauer for not keeping his word. He did not say anyting, but a week later Juta was free. She gave birth to our second son, Michiel, on June 23rd, 1943.

We, of course, knew nothing of all this at the time, other than that they had been caught and that the Nazis were hot on our trail. It gave us one more good reason to quickly make our very own route to Switzerland operational.

THE COURIERS

I saw Van Heuven Goedhart and reported on my discussions with Hans Warendorf. He duly put us in touch with Bosch van Rosenthal who was very co-operative and gave us a password and code names – Henk 301 and Jan 303 – that would give us access to his brother in Bern. He also pumped us full of political information that his brother should pass on to the Dutch government in London with the utmost urgency. Van Heuven Goedhart gave us microfilmed copies of all issues of *Het Parool* to date which should also go to London.

We then selected about a dozen urgent cases of Jews to take to Switzerland. Dries and I had realised early on that, if ever we were caught, it was essential to be able to account for what we had been doing where, without compromising others or ourselves and that we should always be able to back up each other's stories. Therefore, before setting out, we would sit down and make up a story to tell the Germans This routine was to save our lives.

On January 6th, 1943, we started our journey with ten refugees. We smuggled them safely to Brussels in small parties and there they were given excellent French I.D. cards through the organisation of Margot Nyst. From there we took them along our route to a number of safe houses in Belfort where we arrived three days later. Dries and I then went to Paul Ruys's, where we had the door slammed in our faces by his wife who was close to hysteria as Paul had been arrested two days earlier. She made very clear that she wanted nothing more to do with *passeurs*!

This really put us in deep trouble. For two solid days Dries and I scoured every little village in the border area, all the way up to Pontarlier, in our search for a *passeur*. We bought enough drinks to sink a battleship, which was courting arrest ourselves, but all to no avail. At our wit's end, we returned with our tail between our legs to Madame Ruys, who had calmed down by then and was even willing to try and get us the address of at least one of the *passeurs*.

She used a method which was as simple as it was startling to our security conscious minds: she told us to come with her to the jail, went to stand below the window of her husband's cell and yelled up to him. Upon his shouted reply she let him know, at the top of her voice, that his friends were there and wanted Henri's phone number. Ruys unhesitatingly bellowed it down to us. We were back in business!

We called Henri, and arranged with him the transport of the refugees. Unfortunately, the delay had caused two of the group to panic, and they tried to get to Switzerland on their own. Both were caught by the German police and deported. Only one survived. The rest was taken by train, in two small groups and on consecutive nights, to Audincourt and from there on foot the 8 odd kilometres to the Swiss border, which they all crossed safely.

Dries and I were in the second group with a Jewish couple, the Speelmans, and their newborn son. The baby had been given a sedative and was peacefully asleep, cradled in a snug rucksack on its father's back. Walking across country over the heavily wooded hillsides made it quite a strenuous trip. A recent snowfall had melted and frozen up again, which made the going treacherous.

About half a mile from the border, Henri signalled us to take cover, as he could hear a German patrol. We froze against the trees and held our breath. Suddenly deprived of the rocking of its cradle, the baby started to moan. The panicked father whispered to Dries to make it shut up, if necessary by force. But, thank heaven, the baby had already dropped off to sleep again.

When Henri gave the all clear, we went on until we saw the lights of the Swiss border post. Henri told the Speelmans to go there and we waited until we had seen them and their baby arrive safely. We knew that the Swiss would not refuse entry to refugee families with children, but we ourselves could not take the risk either of being turned back, or of losing time in custody. We therefore had to cross the border unnoticed by the authorities, and Henri was to take us into Switzerland along an old smugglers route and drop us at a spot from where we would be able to find our own way to Porrentruy, the nearest village.

It was not exactly a Sunday stroll. We were led up hill, down hill, straight across the forest along a trail that was virtually invisible in the dark. The terrain was extremely rough on us although it did not seem to slow down Henri in any way. Dries and I were panting and heaving, desperately trying to keep up with the stiff pace that our guide was setting. Henri could not afford to dawdle, as he had to make absolutely sure that he was back on French soil before dawn. About half an hour later, he stopped and told us that we now had crossed the border, and only had to continue in the direction he pointed out to us until we hit Porrentruy. We shook hands and he melted into the night.

So there we were, on our own, on a cold and slippery hillside, in the middle of an eerie, dark forest, without a path or track or light to guide us. We slithered from tree to tree, more often than not sliding on our backsides through the mud. It was especially hard on poor Dries. I, at least, had the benefit of basic military training, but he soon could hardly put one foot in front of the other.

At last we came to the edge of the forest, and could just make out the first houses of Porrentruy. There was not a single light. I walked in front in search of a hotel or guesthouse, when suddenly I heard a stifled curse, followed by a resounding crash and the sound of shattering glass I looked around and Dries had vanished. He had lost his footing, slipped into a down-hill garden and landed on a greenhouse! Watching him struggle I could not help but roar with laughter, which did nothing to soften the blow to his ego. He swore at me from the bottom of his heart, and finally managed to climb back onto the road. We hastily continued our search, not keen to hang about and explain to some irate Swiss farmer what had happened to his tomatoes!

The first three hotels we came upon, had a "closed" sign, but at the fourth one we were lucky. After we had leant on the doorbell for a while, a light appeared at a top floor window and a sleepy voice shouted down, what the hell we wanted at this unholy hour. We shouted up that we needed a room. A little while later the door was opened by a man in pyjamas, who reeled back when he saw the state we were in. However, when we explained that we had walked across from France, his expression softened and without a word he let us in. It turned out that this man, who never told us his name, was the owner of the hotel, and a Frenchman whose feelings for the Nazis closely matched our own. When we had taken off our muddy shoes he showed us a most welcoming double room, where he presented us with a laundry basket for our filthy clothes, a few packets of Players cigarettes, and a stiff drink. We soothed our aching limbs under a hot shower, slipped between the spotless sheets, and fell into a dreamless sleep.

We woke up to what seemed a fairytale. Reluctantly answering the persistent knocking, I opened the door to a crisply dressed chambermaid, carrying a huge tray full of goodies, which smelled as if sent straight from Fantasia. We fell to like ravenous wolves. To the delight of Dries, the news-starved journalist, there was also a Swiss newspaper which he devoured hungrily, while at the same time trying, unsuccessfully, to stuff his mouth with food and drink his coffee without spilling it.

However, this was not a holiday, we had work to do! First of all, Dries telephoned the Dutch Embassy in Bern, gave the password for the Ambassador and told him where we were. We were instructed to get on the train to Bienne, where we would be met at the station restaurant by a certain Heytink, one of the embassy staff, to whom we could hand the sensitive material we were carrying and who would give us further instructions.

When, the night before, our wonderful host had asked us how long we would be staying, we had only told him that we had to get to Bern as quickly as possible. We were amazed to find that he had not only gone to the station to get us tickets but had even thought to provide us with the sort of clothes worn by the locals! As a foreigner in Switzerland himself, he had to be extra careful not to get mixed up in anything that might backfire and spell serious trouble if it could be traced back to him by the police. He was therefore doubly keen to make sure that we should get to Bern safely without attracting undue attention.

Anyway, thanks to his precautionary measures, we got to Bienne unchallenged and found Heytink to whom, after he had shown us his credentials, we handed our secret material. He told us that, to circumvent the stringent policecontrol at the Central Station in Bern, we should take the local train, get off at the last stop before the terminal, and go from there by tram to the Ambassador's Residence.

ABOVE Henk Pelser as a medical student.

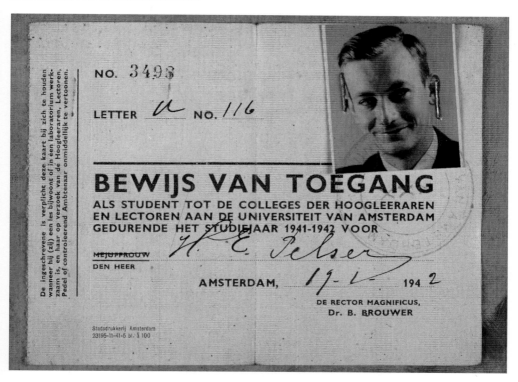

NO. 3493

LETTER *u* NO. *116*

BEWIJS VAN TOEGANG

ALS STUDENT TOT DE COLLEGES DER HOOGLEERAREN
EN LECTOREN AAN DE UNIVERSITEIT VAN AMSTERDAM
GEDURENDE HET STUDIEJAAR 1941-1942 VOOR

~~MEJUFFROUW~~
DEN HEER

AMSTERDAM,   194 *2*

DE RECTOR MAGNIFICUS,
Dr. B. BROUWER

Stadsdrukkerij Amsterdam
23195-11-41-5 bl. á 100

De ingeschrevene is verplicht deze kaart bij zich te houden
wanneer hij (zij) een les bijwoont of in een laboratorium werk-
zaam is, en haar op verzoek van de Hoogleeraren, Lectoren,
Pedel of controleerend Ambtenaar onmiddellijk te vertoonen.

ABOVE Henk Pelser's student card, 1942.

ABOVE "Carnation Day"
– the celebrations for Prince
Bernhard's birthday used by the
Dutch to display their defiance
of the Nazis.

LEFT Saartje Oudkerk, 1940.

RIGHT Police ticket for
breaking curfew.

R REICHSKOMMISSAR
E BESETZTEN NIEDERLÄNDISCHEN GEBIETE

R GENERALKOMMISSAR
R DAS SICHERHEITSWESEN
V B - B.Nr. 5987/41
A'Stwlle Amsterdam

DEN HAAG, den   9. März 1942

B e s c h e i d.

Herrn

Hendrik Emile P e l s e r

A m s t e r d a m

Prinsengracht 393

Auf Grund der §§ 1, Abs. 2, und 5, Abs. 2, der Verordnung des Reichskommissars für die besetzten niederländischen Gebiete vom 29.5.1940 wird Ihnen hiermit eine Geldbusse in Höhe von

hfl 20.-- (zwanzig)

zahlbar bis zum 20.3.1942 auf das Konto der Oberkasse des Reichskommissars bei der Rotterdamschen Bankvereinigung, Den Haag, auferlegt.

Grund:

Sie wurden am 20.2.1942 nach der angeordneten Sperrzeit auf einer öffentlichen Straße in Amsterdam angetroffen und haben damit gegen die Anordnung des Generalkommissars für das Sicherheitswesen für die besetzten niederlän- dischen Gebiete vom 1.2.1942 verstoßen.

In Vertretung:
Der Befehlshaber der Sicherheitspolizei
und des SD.

.d.R.d.A.

Winkelmann

S.-Sturmbannführer

Harster

44-Standartenführer u. Oberst der Polizei.

HET PAROOL

VRIJ ONVERVEERD

VOORJAARSOFFENSIEF
Ons aandeel in den strijd.

In de dagen die achter ons liggen, heeft zich over de voornaamste overzeesche gebiedsdeelen van ons Rijk hetzelfde noodlot voltrokken als over ons eigen land: na een fellen en dapperen strijd moesten ons leger en onze marine voor de overmacht zwichten en zijn de voornaamste gebieden van Nederlandsch-Indië door Japansche troepen bezet.

Er zijn velen, die na den Duitschen inval en bezetting van ons land, zich bewust van de steeds grooter wordende moeilijkheden, die zich als een net om het Duitsche barbarendom sluiten, geen oogenblik getwijfeld hebben aan de tijdelijkheid van deze Duitsche bezetting en alle gevolgen daarvan. Alle teekenen wijzen op de komende ineenstorting van de Teutoonsche overheersching van Europa en daarmee de bevrijding van alle volkeren, die thans vervolgd worden onder het nazi-bewind.

Het bewustzijn, dat het grootste en economisch ook het belangrijkste deel van ons Rijk vrij was van vijandelijken druk en dat daar alle krachten werden ingespannen om mede te werken aan den bevrijdingsstrijd in Europa, wekte hier te lande vertrouwen en hield den moed erin.

Nu Indië voorloopig ook gekneveld ligt onder den druk van den Japanschen bezetter noemen velen Indië verloren en schijnen zij een deel van hun veerkracht kwijt te zijn. Wij weten niet, of er verband bestaat tusschen de verliezen, die ons Rijk in het Verre Oosten heeft geleden en de inzinking, die allerwege in ons land te bespeuren is waar het er om gaat, het verzet tegen den vijand levendig te houden, wat op het oogenblik noodzakelijker is dan ooit, omdat wellicht binnenkort of binnen korteren termijn dan wij kunnen weten de paraatheid en waakzaamheid van het Nederlandsche volk grooter effect zal kunnen sorteeren dan gedurende de bijna twee jaar van Duitsche bezetting het geval is geweest.

Voorloopig richt zich een deel van de teleurstelling over den afloop van den strijd in Indonesië tegen onze bondgenooten. IJverig gevoed door „onze" corrupte pers praat men de Duitschers na inzake de ijdele beloften en laffe vlucht van Engelschen en Amerikanen en speelt men aldus de Duitsche propaganda in de kaart.

Inderdaad, het schouwspel, dat de strijd rondom den Stillen Oceaan ons tot nog toe heeft geboden, is verre van fraai, en voor scherpe critiek is zelfs de Nederlandsche Luitenant Gouverneur-Generaal Van Mook niet teruggedeinsd, maar het kanker, die gelukkig reeds in afnemende mate hier dikwijls te beluisteren viel, kwam in het bijzonder van diegenen, die vaak zelf te lamlendig zijn om hier tot eenig daadwerkelijk verzet te komen en die van meening zijn, dat onze bondgenooten nu maar de kastanjes voor ons uit het vuur moeten halen. En bovendien zijn zij zelf in even groote mate als Amerikanen en Engelschen mede-verantwoordelijk voor het voorloopig falen van de A.B.C.D.-mogendheden in het Verre Oosten. Want in dit falen wreken zich duidelijker dan

waar dan ook in deze wereldworsteling de fouten van het verleden, fouten gemaakt zoowel door ons zelf als door onze bondgenooten.

Evenmin als in Europa na het aan de macht komen van Hitler hebben de democratische landen in het Verre Oosten tijdig het gevaar ingezien, dat werd geschapen door de aanwezigheid van één enkelen agressieven staat als Japan. Jarenlang heeft men het Chineesche volk in zijn worsteling tegen den Japanschen aanvaller geen of nauwelijks hulp geboden, onder het voorwendsel, dat men „neutraal" tegenover beide landen stond. Men heeft, terwijl Japan zijn bewapening voortdurend hooger opvoerde, vooral in de Nederlandsche gebieden tot enkele jaren geleden, toen het echter al te laat was, de defensie verwaarloosd, en tenslotte de ergste fout, die Engeland zoowel als Nederland heeft begaan: men heeft verzuimd, gehoor te geven aan den roepstem van de ontwakende volksgroepen in de koloniale landen, toen deze om grooter vrijheid en bepaalde vormen van zelfbestuur vroegen. Door tijdig hierop in te gaan had men kunnen medewerken aan de bevordering van de ontwikkeling dezer landen, men had de samenwerking op velerlei gebied voor lange jaren kunnen verzekeren, men zou de mogelijkheid hebben gehad, in deze landen massale volkslegers op de been te brengen, die de Japansche indringers zouden hebben bestreden met een elan, waarover slechts jonge volken beschikken, die hun pas verworven vrijheid te verdedigen hebben.

En als Engeland en Amerika op het oogenblik, dat zulks in het Verre Oosten noodig was, niet over de middelen beschikten om de Japansche overmacht weerstand te bieden, dan treft de critiek, die men daarop zou willen oefenen, niet in de eerste plaats Churchill of Roosevelt, noch de Engelsch-Amerikaansche admiraliteit en legerleiding, maar allen, die in de laatste tien jaren verantwoordelijk zijn geweest voor het rustig laten voortbestaan van de stemming van zelfgenoegzaamheid en laksheid, waaruit het totalitaire geweld de democratische landen zoo hardnekkig heeft opgeschrikt.

Het spreekt vanzelf, dat de daardoor ontstane achterstand niet in een vloek en een zucht kan worden ingehaald. Zij, die zich bij deze oude geestesgesteldheid het behaaglijkst hebben gevoeld en het vurigst verlangen naar de terugkeer van den ouden tijd, hebben nu het meeste haast en uiten het luidst op ontevreden toon hun misnoegen en hun ongeduld over het langzame tempo, waarin de anderen aan hun bevrijding werken.

Er zal inderdaad ook bij onze bondgenooten wel heel wat oud vooroordeel moeten worden opgeruimd en heel wat oude figuren — ongetwijfeld goedwillend, maar te zeer verworteld in het verleden — zullen vervangen moeten worden, alvorens de noodzakelijke radicaliseering effectief kan worden. Een radicaliseering, die materiaal zal leiden tot versterking van de strijdkrachten en versnelling van het tempo tot hetzelfde dynamische rythme, waartoe de fascistische horden in staat bleken, en moreel tot de formuleering van de vernieuwingen op economisch, so-

Aardappelen 44	Aardappelen 45	Aardappelen 46	Aardappelen 47	Aardappelen 48	VOEDINGSMI
					11e EN 12e PERIC
ALGEMEEN 256	ALGEMEEN 261	ALGEMEEN 266	ALGEMEEN 271	ALGEMEEN 276	RESERVE B95	RESER B9
ALGEMEEN 257	ALGEMEEN 262	ALGEMEEN 267	ALGEMEEN 272	ALGEMEEN 277	RESERVE B96	RESER B9
ALGEMEEN 258	ALGEMEEN 263	ALGEMEEN 268	ALGEMEEN 273	ALGEMEEN 278	BROOD 48 A	BROO 47 A
ALGEMEEN 259	ALGEMEEN 264	ALGEMEEN 269	ALGEMEEN 274	ALGEMEEN 279	BROOD 48 A	BROO 47 A
ALGEMEEN 260	ALGEMEEN 265	ALGEMEEN 270	ALGEMEEN 275	ALGEMEEN 280	BROOD 48 A	BROO 47 A

ABOVE Food coupons.

ABOVE A *razzia*, or round up, underway in Amsterdam.

LEFT Henk's forged ID card.

BELOW Mau and Siet Frenkel
view their Promised Land
– Switzerland.

TOP LEFT G. Dick van Stokkum,
drawn by Henk Pelser.

TOP RIGHT B. Matthieu Smedts.

BOTTOM RIGHT Ward Messer.

BOTTOM LEFT A. Dries Ekker.

ABOVE Frans Goedhart.

V
IN SWITZERLAND

MISSION ACCOMPLISHED

The Dutch ambassador, a stout man who closely resembled his brother, received us warmly. He complimented us on having managed to evade the Swiss police so far and told us not to show ourselves outside until we had been fully debriefed. That night he treated us to a delicious dinner and a choice selection from his superb wine cellar. He asked us to tell him about the current situation in Holland and it was very apparent that he did not have the vaguest idea what life was like under the German occupation.

The next morning we were completely debriefed and, still at the Ambassador's Residence, were introduced to a number of British MI6 agents, one of whom appeared to be particularly interested in military positions in Holland. Dries could give him information on the situation around the Moerdijk bridge, a strategically important crossing over the Rhine estuary, and I could tell him that one of the main German anti-aircraft batteries in Amsterdam was located right in the historic centre, on top of the Carlton Hotel. It was most satisfying to hear, only a few weeks later, that this battery had been taken out by a single British bomb dropped with such precision that hardly a window rattled in the surrounding canal houses! Dries also had an in-depth interview on the actual situation in Holland with the American reporter Howard Smith, the future anchorman of ABC-TV.

When all that had been done, the Ambassador finally got around to pay his dues to the Swiss authorities and phoned the police to report the arrival of "two Dutch refugees". As the Swiss knew, of course, that we would already have spilled all our beans, they had no interest in us anymore. We were told to report to the *Fremdenstube Zur Heimat* in Gerechtigkeitsgasse, a transit hostel for refugees. We registered there on January 16th, 1943, and found a choice group of residents, mainly impressively bearded Poles and other escapees from Nazi occupied territories, whose principal occupation seemed to be dissecting the current game of chess.

Having registered with the Swiss police, we could now move around freely. We went to the Embassy proper and discussed, in particular with the military attaché, the General Van Tricht, how we could best get back to Holland quickly. Van Tricht and his staff made all the right noises, but appeared to find an obstacle around every corner. However, before we could make any plans, the Swiss suddenly transferred us to a refugee camp at the village of Cossonay, north of Lausanne.

This camp was full of Dutchmen and, as luck would have it, we suddenly stumbled across the Frenkels, who were as delighted as we were at this most unexpected meeting.

THE FRENKELS' STORY

We had a lot to talk about, of course, as I wanted to hear all the gory details of the way they had managed to get to Switzerland after I had left them at the station in De Wildert. Their incredible story follows here in Mau's own words:

In Brussels we were to contact Cox and Daan van der Putten. Cox was a schoolfriend of Henk's fiancée Saartje Oudkerk, and Daan was the Philips representative in Belgium. Through blacked-out Brussels we eventually arrived at their flat Rue Jules le Jeune where we found a warm reception, a bed and, of all things (in 1942!), cornflakes for breakfast! As the tenant of one of the other flats in the building was a Rexist, a Belgian Nazi, we then moved to the Hôtel Mirabeau, Place Brouckère. As the rooms here were rented by the hour – to which the state of the bedclothes clearly testified – for the management to check I.D. cards would obviously be bad for business, which made it a highly suitable address for us fugitives. Daan advised us to give our brand new and squeaky-clean I.D. cards a good rub on a bit of old wooden flooring to give them the patina that goes with long and intensive use.

We had no luck in finding a passeur for the next leg of our trip, and were stuck in Brussels. We went to see Piet Verheul, a friend of our parents and the Belgian representative of the Dutch distillery Hulstkamp. He and his wife had no idea as to what was going on in Holland. We obviously had a lot to tell them and they made sure that our throats were never in danger of drying out. Quite a shock to the system after two abstemious years in occupied Holland! We ended the evening fantastically recklessly in a red plush night club dancing to the dulcet tones of the famous Sten Brender's band!

The next day Piet Verheul told us that he knew someone who helped people escape to Switzerland. As this chap had a passeur leaving with a client the very next day, we had to make up our minds immediately. The "someone", Maurice Loopuit, turned out to be a distant relative of my mother's. A very nice and dapper man with a charming wife. There was hope again!

That night my brother stayed at the house of the passeur, René Poupart, who was a large, massively built man in his early forties, wearing an impeccable double-breasted pin striped suit, pocket-handkerchief showing, and spotless patent leather shoes. He had dark, slicked back hair and, as a result of his sometime career as a boxer, a nose that was slightly out of true – in short, a man who, in the circumstances, inspired us with the utmost confidence!

I myself spent that night at the Hôtel des Colombes, near the Brussels North railway station. The hotel was full of German soldiers, which meant that all rooms had double occupancy! When, in the middle of the night, pandemonium broke out amongst this motley crew as a result of an air raid alarm, I thought it safer to stay in my bed rather than join my fellow residents in the cellar.

In the morning I bought emergency rations consisting of a good supply of sugared almonds – these were not rationed as they were traditionally used at first communion services! – and then went to meet Poupart and my brother at the Gare de Luxembourg, a railway station that resembled nothing as much as a mini Crystal Palace.

We took the train to Paliseul, a small town in the Ardennes, and spent the time getting to know René Poupart. He had installed himself comfortably with his feet on the upholstered seat across, but not before he had neatly spread a newspaper to receive them – a custom which today seems to have gone out of fashion even in the First Class carriages! Poupart had lived in Chicago for many years. It never became clear what brought him there, but it was obvious that the reasons for him to leave had been most compelling. The three of us got on very well and even developed something akin to friendship. In Paliseul we changed to a real old-fashioned narrow gauge train, still drawn by a steam engine, which took us through dense Ardennes forests in the cheerful company of local peasants, all in their Sunday best, with wicker baskets which were soon shown to contain quantities of fried drumsticks and other delicacies.

In Bouillon we went to a most comfortable restaurant where we partook of a refreshing glass of Spa water while awaiting the next link in our journey. In the distance we could suddenly hear something that sounded like a chainsaw in trouble: "Ah, c'est mon ami!", said Poupart. And indeed, within minutes we met the friend, known as Frère Jacques, who was to drive us to Sedan in his motorcar.

Customs formalities as the Belgian-French border were simple and swiftly dealt with: Poupart handed over a quantity of cigarettes and some new bicycle tires which, obviously, had been ordered on a previous occasion. We were then free to continue our journey to Sedan where Poupart went to change some money in a café on the market square. The square itself looked most bizarre. The German attack, two years previously, had virtually obliterated the centre of Sedan and the only bits left standing of the buildings around the square were a *few pieces of wall with empty window frames. In the middle of this rubble stood a merry-go-round and other paraphernalia of the annual fair. Ruins and fairground alike were starkly silhouetted against a black sky, while music blasted all around in the colourless stillness of an impending thunderstorm.*

Early in the morning Poupart, ourselves and Wessels, the original client who had been with us since Brussels, again assembled at the railway station. We took what was supposed to be the fast train to Nancy but, due to shortages, even these trains were slow and the trip took most of the day. As Nancy was not in a restricted border area, it was possible to get a hotel room without permission of the German administration and apparently even forged Belgian papers were sufficient identification. We stayed at the Hôtel du Cerf, a wonderful creaky timber inn. We dined at Le Tout Va Bien: nomen est omen! An old-fashioned French establishment, "pain et vin à discretion", and delicious field mushrooms in cream sauce. We surreptitiously stuffed our pockets full of bread. Even the fact that the rest of the clientele consisted largely of fat German Brownshirts with swastika armbands did not spoil our appetite. It seemed safe to assume, if only on purely physiological grounds, that an SA-man with a scantily clad lady on his lap – and that went for all of them – was not going to be a threat to us.

After a good night's sleep and a glass of coffee at the station, we continued our trip to Belfort where a contact of Poupart would meet us in the café across from the station. But there was no one there. Poupart, natural débrouillard (fixer) as he was, soon beamed in to another passeur loitering in the station, who told him that the Belfort-Switzerland route had been blown and that the regular passeurs had been arrested and executed. It was then arranged that, the next day, this man would take us across the border via Besançon. As Belfort was in the restricted zône, we had to return to Nancy to spend the night and Poupart returned to Brussels.

In the early morning we took the train to Besançon, a much longer journey. The train was packed out with Jewish refugees, some Dutch but also many from Antwerp where razzias had been held recently. The latter were mainly originally Polish Jews, most of who were in the diamond or fur trade. In our compartment we met a very charming biology student from Antwerp with her parents and ancient, rather decrepit, grandparents. Once the door of the compartment was jerked open. A check by the Feldgendarmerie. "Sind Juden da?" (Any Jews?). Without waiting for an answer the door was slammed shut and the official moved on to the next compartment. The corridor of the train was packed with refugees and the windows were wide open to the beautiful weather. One of the passengers was overheard to say to his wife in the broadest Amsterdam dialect: "This is Belfort station" whereupon she snapped: "Don't be daft, this is only Sortie"! At one of the stations we spotted a cheerful, rucksacked lady, Mrs. Wolff-Gerzon, whom we had so rudely abandoned in Essen.

In Besançon we met the passeur from Belfort as arranged, and he took the three of us and the biology student and her family to the Café du XXième Siècle, on the edge of town. Our reception there was less than courteous and we were told to wait in a dingy room behind the taproom, obviously the storage for the musical instruments of the local brass band. When the student finally asked the landlady when she thought somebody would come for us, she got a curt: "Ta gueule, sale Juive!" (Shut up, filthy Jew!). This did nothing to improve our already flagging spirits!

Eventually, late in the afternoon, a man appeared whose looks already did not inspire me with much confidence. Skinny, a wrinkled face with ferrety dark eyes. It immediately brought to my mind the quote from Julius Caesar: "Yon Cassius hath a lean and hungry look – such men are dangerous". We were quickly loaded into an old, decrepit taxi and ordered to hand over all our money. Fortunately, I had taken the precaution to hide a sizeable amount of Swiss Francs amongst my clothing and this, at least, I was able to keep.

We sped along narrow, dirty country lanes, over hills and through forests, a rather eerie drive. The biology student asked where he was taking us, a legitimate question, to which she got the shocking reply: "Shut up, or I will take you straight to the Gestapo!" Finally we arrived at a remote farm, where the driver told us to "get out and hurry, This is it!" "Are we in Switzerland??" Without giving us an answer he turned around and drove off in a cloud of dust. We had been robbed! But where were we?

"La Brétenière" turned out to be a hamlet on the German side of the border with unoccupied France. The farm was a staging post on the route used by French and Polish POWs who had escaped from German camps. There was a woman in charge, very pregnant and very skinny. We were given a place to sleep in the attic together with some escaped Polish POWs. We seemed to be stuck here. A passeur would not take us as we had no money and the only other option appeared to be to join the Foreign Legion. Fortunately, we did not think this a terribly attractive idea anyway, as it was open to any scoundrel under the sun, but would not take any Jews.

A man with a racing bicycle appeared. About 30 years old, he had an honest face and told us that he worked in the Besançon abattoir. His name was Raymond. When I told him about our unfortunate experience with the cabdriver, he said we had better come to his home in Besançon to figure out what to do. He seemed such a nice and ostensibly decent man, that my brother and I thought we could do worse than follow his suggestion.

At crack of dawn we set out and walked cross country for about an hour to the tiny station of Orchamp where we took the daily (!) train to Besançon. The little train looked as though it was straight out of a Monet painting and on its gentle jog through the countryside was a perfect illustration of Marcel Proust's tortillard. The only other passengers were some peasant women going to market to sell their wares and some hunters toting guns and bags.

In Besançon we found Raymond at the Municipal Slaughterhouse where he was the foreman. He lived over the abattoir with his lovely wife and two little girls, Yvonne and Michèle. Raymond had been a racing cyclist before the war and told us proudly that he had competed in the Tour de France a few times. We discussed our options over a delicious and, by now, very welcome cassoulet full of great chunks of juicy meat. Although we knew that it was very dangerous, we decided that we had to return to Brussels in order to replenish our funds. Raymond lent us some French Francs to pay the fare and we left our Swiss Francs with him as security.

We spent the night in the stables of the local fire brigade, and the next day took the train to Brussels. The journey was interrupted frequently and we spent a lot of time in sundry waiting rooms. At a station bookstall we bought, less out of political affinity than for purposes of camouflage, recent issues of the popular German wartime weeklies Adler (Eagle) and Angriff (Attack). The display of these blatant Nazi propaganda rags effectively silenced any conversation amongst our fellow-passengers. Our meals consisted only of weak beer and small but sweet white grapes which were for sale everywhere. Not unexpectedly, there was an I.D. check at the French-Belgian border at Givet. The Military Policeman did this by assuming a stern frown, looking at our (forged) papers, then at us, then again at our papers, trying hard to look frightfully intimidating. As we were far too tired to care, we passed the test with flying colours!

In Brussels, Maurice Loopuit was shocked by our reappearance and immediately arranged with Poupart to take us to Besançon a second time. The Loopuits treated us to a delightful warm bath and a visit to the most fashionable hairdresser in Brussels, next to the "temporarily closed" British Embassy. I sent a postcard with a cryptic message to my parents, expecting that it would cause Henk to contact Mathieu Smedts. The description of the escape route, Raymond's address in Besançon and the password: "Yvonne et Michèle" we left with Cox and Daan van der Putten to pass on to Henk.

Our next trip to Besançon was uneventful but for the news that only a few days after we were there last the Gestapo had raided "La Brétenière". We later heard that the pregnant farmer's wife had been executed by the Nazis after the baby that was born to her in prison had died.

The next day Raymond took us, via Mouchard, to La Joux, a tiny little station in the middle of the forest and left us there to wait for our passeur. The French Resistance seemed to know exactly which stations were being patrolled by the Germans and when; La Joux, today, was apparently free of patrols. We had arrived at 9 a.m. and sat there and waited all day, eating bread and hard boiled eggs that we had brought from Brussels.

Mid-morning, another train arrived which disgorged large numbers of basket-toting children who were going to search for berries in the forest. A man also got out of this train, in his thirties, squat and very muscular. His name was René Poitevin. He told us that he was a French army officer who had been made a POW by the Germans in 1940 and that he had spent two years in a rather grim

Stalag. In preparations for an escape attempt, the inmates had secretly made compass needles out of razorblades. This was discovered and he was moved to another camp for punishment. During the transport there, he managed to overpower his guards and jumped off the train. He headed West and walked for days through dense German forests, living on snails and the odd chicken poached off a farmyard and eaten raw. Not far from the Rhine, which he had to cross, he ambushed a hapless farmer and was then able to continue his journey in the farmer's clothes, with his money still in his pockets and on his victim's bicycle. What happened to the farmer I never dared ask, but it cannot have been very pleasant.

Now looking like a local, he simply biked across the Rhine bridge at Breisach near Freiburg, gave the guards a wave and a cheery "Heil Hitler" and was back in his beloved France. He desperately needed new shoes (the farmer obviously had been unable to oblige!) and to this end went to the priest in the first village he came across. Monsieur le Curé (who happened to have the right size!) gave him his spare pair of regulation shoes with black pom-poms and this is what René was wearing when he arrived at La Joux station. He was hungry and cold. We gave him a spare woollen sweater we had and shared our bread and cold eggs with him. The three of us spent all day on this lone little station and talked, waiting for the train that would bring our passeur and the rest of the group going to unoccupied France.

It was early evening when they finally arrived. Two passeurs accompanied the little group: a man, whom I cannot recall, and a very beautiful young woman, Paulette: charming but businesslike. She was wearing an incredible coat, reversible, black on one side, white on the other. She knew exactly which colour to wear against which background to make herself totally invisible – a remarkable and very useful accomplishment!

All of us – we were now a group of 8 or 9 – had to pass a sort of test to prove that we were genuine. Raymond had already warned us about this and also about the fact that Dutch Jews were not high on the favourite persons list of the French Resistance. So Siet and I had prepared ourselves to impersonate a couple of medical students from Ghent in Belgium, which was most

85

successful. We then received a number of instructions. The first was to make as little noise as possible on our ten hour hike through the forest – no rustling leaves, no stepping on dry wood, no talking, anything that could rattle had to be secured to the extent that we had to put cottonwool in our matchboxes to keep the matches still! In order not to lose each other in the pitch-dark forest, we each had to pin a white handkerchief to our shoulder for the person behind us to follow.

We walked for hours and hours and managed to keep going on the caffeine powders we had brought from Holland. Eventually we came to a clearing where we crossed the main road and then the railway line. That was quite a business, as not only did the Germans patrol the line regularly with one of those little hand-moved carts, but they also were said to have listening devices attached to the rails that would betray the slightest noise. So we couldn't walk on the gravel and could not touch the rails and had to do a sort of tight-rope walk across the sleepers. Then we were carried across a small river and were in unoccupied France!

We walked across a wide open plain, heading for a tiny speck of light in the distance. This turned out to be a farm, called "La Hollande" of all things, and obviously a hotbed of Resistance activities. We arrived there at about 5 a.m. and inside, clustered around the little light, found a group of people sitting at a wooden table, drinking coffee in one of those typically French farmhouse kitchens full of shadows and dark recesses. We all got a mug of coffee and our passeurs the latest information and when the sun started rising we set off again along a seemingly endless dirt trail.

At last we came to a bus stop and there we finally caught the bus, first to Champagnole, a little east of Crotenay, and from there another bus to Lons le Saunier. A French policeman came on board to inspect I.D. cards. He looked at ours and gave them back but, to our horror, returned a little later and told us that our papers were forgeries, that we had to hand them over and report to the Commissariat Spécial at Lons le Saunier. And there we saw him again, this policeman, Monsieur Meyer – may he burn in hell – sitting behind a high desk in his office, ordering us to report to the Foyer des Rapatriés. There we found a nice bunch of people, most of them escaped POWs. Also there was a 16-year old Dutch boy, Roelof de Haan, who had been so afraid to face his rather stern mother and even fiercer grandmother with the miserable marks on his school report – particularly his French was lousy! – that he had decided to abscond from his home in Leeuwarden, in the far north of The Netherlands, and had bicycled all the way to Lons le Saunier! The sum total of his knowledge of French amounted to the words manger (to eat) and coucher (to sleep) and with those he had managed perfectly well, scrounging food and lodging from likely looking farms. He decided to attach himself to us which we did not mind as he really was a nice boy, a little childish perhaps, with a rather excessive sense of adventure. Unfortunately, life in the Swiss camps had a bad influence on him and he eventually submerged into a life of crime. A shame really, he would have done better to stay with his mum, bad marks and all.

At the Foyer des Rapatriés we were put under house arrest. When we were being registered we had to state our religion. When we said that we were Lutheran they refused to believe me. They believed Siet, who looked less Jewish, but not me and when I insisted they told me that I would have to go through a medical inspection! Not a happy prospect!

The next morning, out on our daily trip to get our ration cards, we ran into René Poitevin. He said: "The most ridiculous thing just happened to me, you won't believe it! Just imagine, I happened to be at the Commissariat Spécial and ran into that man Meyer who asked me if I knew anything about "those two Jewish blokes". "Jewish blokes?" I said, "those two? I give you my word as an officer and a gentleman that they are not Jews! They cannot be! They shared their food with me and gave me a sweater when I was cold – trust me, they are certainly no Jews!" The word of honour of a French officer proved to be enough for Meyer, and we were left in peace!

We received a message from the Préfet Départemental, a Monsieur Chataigne, to report to him. We went to see him and he received us most cordially.

"Are you Dutch?"

"Yes, we are."

"You do realise that your I.D. cards are not really any good, don't you? You had better get rid of them! I will get you some travel documents because it is terribly important that you go to Lyon and see your Consul as soon as possible."

This was very, very odd, as there was no Dutch Consul in Lyon during the war. But we did not complain, got our papers and ration cards for bread, cigarettes and sweets. M. Chataigne gave us a firm handshake and said: "Bon voyage et bonne chance!" He added: "Don't take the main entrance to the station but go into the station restaurant, get yourselves a cup of coffee or a beer and when the train comes, go directly onto the platform through the restaurant exit. You will be all right then."

Just outside Chataigne's office, his secretary came up to us and said: "Good thing that you are not Jewish, because there are big razzias in Lyon at the moment, all Jews are being rounded up. I just thought that you would like to know this, although you, of course, have nothing to worry about." Her name was Mademoiselle Bloch, hence her concern! Obviously, everybody in that Préfecture was in the Résistance!

And so, on September 9th, 1942, we went to Lyon where we arrived late in the afternoon, after the close of business. The next day we found the Office Néerlandais. This was a, totally unofficial, private little office, rum by a man called Jacquet who was also in the Resistance and had made it his job to disperse false papers. He was assisted by Sally Noach, a Jewish refugee from Amsterdam, and between the two of them they helped countless people, at great risk to themselves and with no thought of personal gain at all. Sally gave us new I.D. cards, warning us that they were not really any good, but better than nothing at all. We were told to take the train to Annecy and to jump out just before the Annecy tunnel where the train would be going very slowly. But, as I said to Siet, I did not think that that was a very good plan because, if Sally Noach knew that that was a good place to jump off, the Vichy police was bound to know as well!

We got on the train. At one of the stations we saw the Police Noire, the black-uniformed Vichy police, get onto the train to check papers. They boarded at the rear of the train, we got off well ahead of them at the trackside, walked back and boarded again behind them – a trick we had been taught by Henk. It worked every time! We noticed in passing that the place near the tunnel where we were supposed to have abandoned the train, was indeed quite heavily guarded! At around midnight we arrived in Annecy.

Annecy station was also riddled with police, but we were lucky and able to slip through. In a boathouse on the lake we slept like logs.

There was a bus from Annecy to St. Julien, near Geneva, that left at around 10 a.m. Convenient, but also very dangerous as there were strict controls. We went to investigate and actually saw people being picked out of the queue and taken away by the police. We had to come up with a plan!

We walked away from the station, desperately thinking of a way to get on that bus. We passed a bakery and my mind's eye suddenly focussed on some fancy apricot tarts in the window. Huge, sweet, sticky tarts, with pink glaze lettering that said: Pour Ma Tante. They were covered by an army of wasps that clearly found them highly attractive. "Guys", I said, "this is it!" And the three of us, Roelof de Haan, Siet and I, went in and – with the coupons we had been given by kind Mr. Chataigne – we each bought a tart, each tart with its private swarm of wasps firmly attached.

I hate wasps. They absolutely terrify me. But the thought of a concentration camp proved to be a great antidote!

Armed with our tarts we walked back to the bus, looking for all the world like three kind young men taking their mum's home baked for a Sunday treat to a dear old aunt living in the next village. We walked straight up to the bus, went in and sat down, careful not to disturb our little winged friends in their orgy of gluttony. Nobody ever asked to see our papers. Probably terrified of wasps too! This was, without a doubt, the greatest stroke of genius I have ever had in my life.

The bus duly left and an hour later we were in Abbaye le Pommier, a small village near the Swiss border. We got off the bus and ate the tarts. They were very good! We had bought a large-scale map and a compass. Our route lay along the foot of Mont Salève. We set off and, after walking for a few hours, we could see a blue stripe in the distance – the Lake of Geneva! And near it, a small white blob – the building of the League of Nations. I felt like Moses seeing the Promised Land! But it was still a long way off and, however much we walked, it did not seem to get much closer.

It was already towards the end of the afternoon when we met some woodcutters, local Savoyards, who asked if we happened to have any cigarettes. We distributed my last packet of Lucky Strikes and their next question was if we were Gaullists. "Yes", we said, and they immediately claimed us as brothers. "We want to go to Switzerland," we ventured. "No problem" they said, "but please, come and eat with us first and then we will take you across!" They took us to a cabin, a hovel in the forest, where we were filled up with thick cassoulet and copious quantities of white wine. For dessert a mug of delicious, fresh goat's milk and then, although I felt a little unsteady on my feet, our hosts were ready to leave. "We Savoyards", they said, "usually sing when we are walking. Won't you sing something too?" My mind was not working too clearly and I enthusiastically started "Allons enfants de la patrie........." A large hand was swiftly clamped over my mouth and a gruff voice said: "Whoa, whoa, anything but that!".

After a while we came to a road with a low barbed wire fence on the other side. "If you were to step over that wire you would be in Switzerland", we were told! So we did and were most cordially received by a Mr. Gave, the farmer on whose land we happened to be. He gave us a welcome drink of very young and extremely potent wine and then sent us on our way to Geneva. It wasn't really surprising that it did not take long before the Swiss police spotted us and marched us, "hands up" off to the nearest police post. Siet, also somewhat the worse for wear, got an unstoppable and most undiplomatic fit of the giggles!

We were questioned and eventually sent to Stade de Varanbé, the local soccer stadium, which was packed with refugees. More interrogations and then we were sent to a closed security camp at Geneveys sur Coffrance, a blot on the landscape somewhere high up in the mountains near the French border. Here we stayed for a month.

The most memorable thing that happened was that we suffered a massive *infestation of lice. We all had to go to the municipal bathhouse where we were stripped and deloused and all our clothes were sent to be sterilised. To keep us decent we were lent some clothes – and the only things available in quantity were the costumes of the local amateur theatrical society. We ended up as fifty-odd clowns all stinking of carbolic acid!*

After about a month our status was changed from "Refugee, possible spy" to "Refugee, general category, Dutch" and we were transferred to the work camp at Cossonay.

Dries and I were to discover that life in the Cossonay refugee workcamp was far from comfortable. The pragmatic Swiss had shrewdly located it in a marshy area, which they wanted to drain, and were keeping the refugees usefully occupied as cheap labour.

We rose at crack of dawn and, after a scanty breakfast, collected a pickaxe and went to dig trenches in the frozen soil. As we were not really used to exertion of this kind, our hands, in no time, were covered with blisters. But it did not take us long to find a sneaky way to cut down a bit on the backbreaking work. Whenever the foreman was not looking, we would deftly smash the wooden handle of our pickaxe and then, without any undue haste, stroll back to the tool-shed to collect a new one.

Not only did we have to put up with hard labour, we also had to endure a rather basic diet. On Fridays, we were given jacket potatoes and a piece of Emmenthaler cheese for lunch, supposedly an old Swiss tradition. But on Saturdays and Sundays we were allowed to go out and buy our own meals, which was a welcome treat. I still remember how much we enjoyed our first raclette dinner, to which the Frenkels treated us, and how our wobbly legs and throbbing heads the next day were a painful testimony to our overindulgence in the accompanying kirsch!

THE TRIP BACK

Dries and I had been in the camp for about three weeks, when we were moved out as unexpectedly as we had arrived. We soon found out that this was the doing of the Reverend Visser 't Hooft, then Secretary of the World Council of Churches in Geneva, who had been told about us and that we wanted to go back to Holland. As Visser 't Hooft, was not an accredited diplomat, and a close confidant and trusted advisor of Queen Wilhelmina, he was an excellent go-between for the Resistance and the Dutch Government-in-Exile. He claimed us from the Swiss on the pretext that he needed us to assist him in his ecclesiastical work!

We were put up at the Hôtel International Genève the abode of quite a few refugees who were allowed to live outside the camps as they could pay their own way.

Unlike the two of us, most of them wanted to go to allied countries and were waiting to be channelled into an escape line via Spain and Portugal. We were the odd men out and it was exactly because of this that the Ambassador had brought us to the attention of Visser 't Hooft.

We went to Geneva and were received most kindly. Visser 't Hooft kindly but expertly probed into our background and our motives and then referred us to his assistants, "*oompje*" (little uncle) Van Niftrik and Joop Bartels, who were put in charge of arranging our return to The Netherlands.

In our free time, we had interesting discussions with a Croat we met at the hotel through Tilly Visser, the rather capricious but fascinating daughter of the former President of the Dutch Supreme Court who, being a Jew, had been dismissed by the Nazis, and had recently died before they could deport him.

Tilly's friend appeared to be a fervent supporter of the communist guerrillaleader "Tito" – whom we had never heard of before – who fought the Nazis as fiercely as he did his political rival, the Serb nationalist guerrilla leader Mihailovic, whose name we had actually

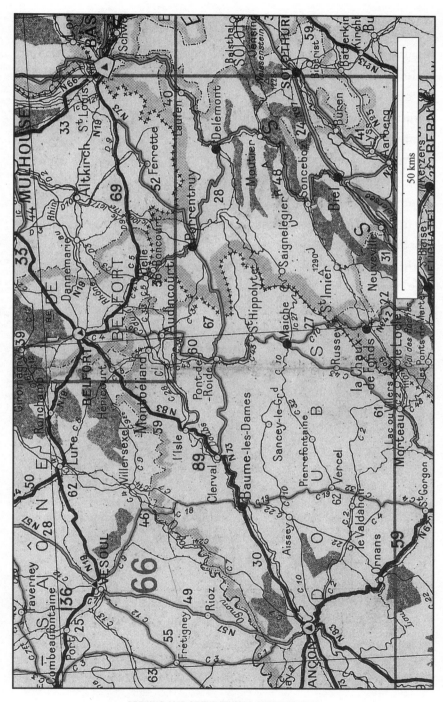

PRE-WAR MAP OF THE FRANCO-SWISS BORDER.

heard being mentioned on the BBC. We had many elaborate discussions on the intricacies of the complicated political, religious, and ethnic situation in the Balkans, which were as incomprehensible to our western democratic minds as his conviction that these traditional rivalries could only be contained by an autocratic communist regime.

We also avidly scoured the newspapers for the latest on the war, and were delighted to read that at the Casablanca meeting Roosevelt and Churchill had decided only to make peace with Germany, Italy, or Japan after their unconditional surrender. The other bit of good new was that the "great and glorious" German Sixth Army had capitulated to the Russians at Stalingrad! From the Pacific battlefront there was little news but we were confident that the Allies would crush the Japanese as soon as the Nazis and the Fascists were brought to their knees. There was still a lot to be fought for!

At last we were given our "battle orders" for the return trip:

1. We were to try to free from the special Nazi prison camp for hostages in Vught (near 's Hertogenbosch in the south-east of the country) Dries's former boss, D.J. Von Balluseck, the Editor-in-Chief of the *Algemeen Handelsblad* (one of the leading pre-war newspapers in Holland), and tell him that the Dutch Government in London urgently wanted him there to run *Radio Oranje* and its broadcasts to The Netherlands;

2. Upon his agreement, we were to bring him to Perpignan where he was to be handed over to two old ladies (whose address and password we had to memorise, of course) who would get him to England via Spain and Portugal;

3. If Von Balluseck were to refuse the job or if it would prove to be impossible to get him out of the camp, we were to offer the assignment to Van Heuven Goedhart. The only reason that the latter was not to be asked first, was because of his importance as one of the leaders of the Resistance. Unlike Von Balluseck, who had

been imprisoned for quite a while, Van Heuven Goedhart's knowledge and contacts were totally up-to-date which made him of greater value to the London government.

4. We were to find out whether a certain airfield in Twente (near the Dutch-German border) was the base for a German nightfighter;

5. To the underground press we were to deliver microfilmed features from recent newspapers and magazines, including the complete text of the Beveridge Plan, which had already been announced in the broadcasts of *Radio Oranje* and had attracted great interest;

6. I was empowered to authorise the Political Convention, a recently established body in the Resistance, to distribute a considerable amount of money for various resistance activities.

7. In return for sharing information, especially on economic aspects, the Swiss authorities had informed their border posts of our code names and instructed them to let us pass in and out of the country.

On Friday afternoon, February 19th, we were taken back to Porrentruy by Joop Bartels, and passed on to officers of the Swiss border police. They took us, together with a man who was said to be a French telegraph operator, to about a mile from the border with France. After dusk we were taken to the border itself by a lean, elderly, but sprightly peasant, who taught us en route how to find the Pole Star from the Great Bear, and navigate on it. At the border he took his leave with an encouraging *"au revoir"*, and disappeared. We quickly crossed the border road and vanished into the forest. The Frenchman proved to be an ace at night-walking, and via Beaucourt we reached Audincourt at about 11 p.m. and found comfortable lodgings for the night.

The next morning, Saturday, Dries and I went to Montbelliard and took the train to Sedan. We arrived there in the afternoon and went to our familiar cafe to find out if it would be possible to get our "frère Jacques" to come from Bouillon and pick us up. This was no problem. "Frère Jacques" had left the cafe only ten minutes ago to take a passenger to the station, and would surely be back soon. He was indeed, but the moment he saw us he threw up his hands in frustration: the passenger he had just put on the train to Belfort was none other than Dick van Stokkum. Dick had got worried about our long absence and decided to go and find out for himself what had happened! As we could not possibly catch up with him any more, we decided to continue our journey.

After the usual bloodcurdling drive to Bouillon we took the train to Brussels and on Saturday evening, only 24 hours after our departure from Switzerland we arrived at our safe address with Margot Nyst.

BACK IN HOLLAND

The next morning we went through the normal routine for a trip to Amsterdam: half an hour before the early Brussels-Amsterdam express was to leave, we got on the train to Antwerp, went by taxi to the cafe in Essen where we always kept our bicycles, rushed to the farm of the Denissen family in Ruecphen, near Roosendaal, quickly exchanged our Belgian I.D. cards for our Dutch ones which were hidden there, and raced to Roosendaal to arrive in time to catch the Brussels-Amsterdam express. A dining car was always provided especially for the German officers in order to alleviate the tedium of the journey, and we usually joined them for a hearty breakfast. About noon on Sunday, less than 48 hours after we had left Geneva, we were back in Amsterdam!

We each went to our own safe house, and started to work on our assignments. We delivered the microfilms and the authorisation for the Political Assembly to Van Heuven Goedhart and Bosch van Rosenthal, respectively, who both debriefed us completely on our experiences in Switzerland. To find out how to get the military information we were to take back to Switzerland on our next trip, we were referred to Bosch van Rosenthal junior in Leiden. He took a lot of persuading before agreeing to collect these and other data for us. In return, he wanted us, as soon as we were back in Switzerland, to see if we could arrange the exchange, against a prisoner of the Allies, of a certain Kees Dutilh. They were very worried about Dutilh who had been arrested for espionage a few days earlier, on March 10th. (He was executed by the Nazis at the end of February 1944!)

We also started trying to get in touch with Von Balluseck. Dries was still an employee of the *Algemeen Handelsblad* and officially on sick-leave because of supposedly serious tuberculosis which was sure to make his colleagues reluctant to visit him! He could therefore, without raising too many eyebrows, enquire after his former boss. He found out that, from time to time, Von Balluseck was allowed to go out of the camp and see his physician in nearby Hertogenbosch. He would then normally also visit his friend Moussault. From the former Secretary of the editorial staff, A.J. Boskamp, who was another good friend of Von Balluseck, Dries managed to get an introduction to Moussault, and went to see him.

At their first meeting Moussault promised Dries that he would put him in touch with Von Balluseck, but somehow there always was a hitch. According to Moussault, who became less and less co-operative, Von Balluseck did not come out any more. Dries was never quite sure what was really behind this. Boskamp had only been willing to co-operate if he knew exactly why Dries wanted to see Von Balluseck. A little later he let slip that he and his (Jewish) wife were about to leave for London themselves, and also hinted rather openly that he was himself interested in the job at *Radio Oranje*. Dries offered to take them to Switzerland as, from Boskamp's stories, he had strong suspicions about the organisation that was supposed to get them to Brussels. But although Boskamp knew very well that we had been to Switzerland, and would soon go there again, he preferred to go his own way. As Dries had feared, the Boskamps were arrested the moment they set out. Mrs Boskamp never came back.

Meanwhile, time to contact Von Balluseck ran out, so we decided to go for plan B. We went to see Van Heuven Goedhart again and put our cards on the table: although the government in London wanted for *Radio Oranje* an editor like him, who was fully acquainted with the situation in The Netherlands it was, at the same time, reluctant to deprive the Resistance of one of its top leaders. But as it had not been possible to get Von Balluseck, we were instructed to offer the job to him and arrange his journey to London via Perpignan.

Van Heuven Goedhart's reaction was totally in character:

"They either want me, or they want Von Balluseck! If they have good reasons for asking him, great! If they want me, they should ask me and only me! When are you going back to Switzerland?"

"If we don't have to take you to Perpignan, on or about the 5th of April", we replied.

"Then go and get them to make up their minds!", Van Heuven Goedhart said.

There was no hesitation, no doubt at all in his reaction! Although it was an unwelcome complication, we certainly could understand his reasoning and at least he had left the door open. He did promise to give us a memorandum setting out his conditions for the London job. Dries and I now quickly started to prepare our next trip to Switzerland.

This also meant getting forged I.D. cards for a small group of people who urgently needed to get away and whom we would take with us. Dick van Stokkum, who was in charge of providing the documents, had promised that they would be ready for Dries to pick up at the *Nieuwe Suyckerhofje* on April 2nd, 1943.

VI
ARRESTED

WE ARE CAUGHT

What happened then is best described by Dries himself:

After dark, I entered the door to the passage that led to the mews. There I passed two people whom I greeted, as I assumed they were residents, although I could not clearly make them out. When I had passed them, they suddenly jumped me. They were Dutch S.D. agents! It turned out that they had been hanging about all day, arresting anybody walking into the mews. I was quickly searched and arrested without charge. Some time later that night a prison van came to take us to Euterpe Street (where the Amsterdam S.D. headquarters were). During the ride I actually managed to get rid of all incriminating documents which had, stupidly enough, been left on me at the initial search. I simply threw them out of the van! But even having done that, and in spite of my nice I.D. card in the name of Nicolaas Witsen, G.P, I was soon found to be the infamous Andries Ekker, a wanted man since early November 1942. This was not a pleasant predicament as Messer, Smedts and some of the others who had already been arrested, all thought that Pelser and I had escaped to Switzerland and had probably saddled us with a host of things which they had rather not explain to the Gestapo themselves. But, apparently, the enormous number of arrests made by the S.D. that night prevented them from prodding me for more information. I was transferred to the detention centre at Weteringschans where I was incarcerated with two Communists who had already been in prison for a long time and had much experience of the German methods of interrogation. One of them, an elderly employee of a slaughterhouse, asked me why I had been arrested. When I said that I had not the faintest idea, he nodded approvingly and told me to make sure that whatever it was I had not done, it was certainly not done out of friendship for Jews! When I asked him why, he explained that the Nazis would consider somebody breaking the law out of greed less culpable than one who was moved by morals and a sense of decency. The latter would be branded as Judenfreund *(friend of the Jews) and his life in prison would be made particularly grim. Eminent advice, to be remembered!*

I knew that Van Stokkum had been arrested. I could only hope that Pelser had managed to keep out of their hands. A few days later I heard, however, that he had also been caught, not a day after I had been arrested, and also at the *Nieuwe Suyckerhofje*.

On April 3rd, I was running a few errands, still in blissful ignorance of what had happened at the mews the day before. I went to deliver a message to one of Dick van Stokkum's sisters and she too had not yet heard of the previous day's fateful events. She mentioned that a new tenant had damaged the façade of one of the little houses at my beloved *Nieuwe Suyckerhofje* by overloading the gable hoist. Fuming with rage at this rank stupidity I rushed over to the Prinsengracht to see for myself what damage had been done.

I stormed through the entrance door and saw that the gate in the passage had been left unlocked, which only added to my fury and, in search of a victim to vent my anger on, I ran straight into the inner court to see if somebody was there. There was! A man in plain clothes wanted to know who I was and what I was looking for. When I explained that I lived there, he told me that I was under arrest and took me directly to Euterpestraat.

I still remember vividly that my first reaction was actually a feeling of relief! This may seem odd, but is, apparently, quite a common reaction for people who, like me, had been active in the Resistance for a relatively lengthy and uninterrupted period of time. Apparently the human mind cannot endure the strain of being continuously on the alert for a period of much more than about six months. After that, errors of judgement start occurring, in my case overlooking the fact that the passage gate had been unlocked and open, a blatant violation of the strict rule that it should be locked shut at all times.

My immediate second reaction to the arrest, however, was a firm resolve to try and manoeuvre myself out of this situation by feigning innocence at any charge that might be laid against me. At the interrogation, therefore, I acted the part of a simple medical student, full of willingness to co-operate and eager to clear up the obvious misunderstanding that had led to my arrest!

The first questions I had to answer were on my acquaintance with Willem Arondeus, and my whereabouts on the night of Saturday, March 27th. Obviously they suspected me of being involved in the raid carried out by the group of Gerrit van der Veen and Willem Arondeus on the Municipal Registration Office. (Note 4) Although I remembered having met Arondeus, I maintained that I had never heard of him and said that I had been out of town for the weekend with a friend, of whom I supplied a (fictitious) name and address.

My interrogator then wanted to know if I had any Jewish friends. I answered that the religion of my friends did not interest me. I was then treated to a lengthy peroration in which he described, in great detail, the many despicable and corrupting character flaws of the Jewish race. When he had finished, I remarked that, as a student of anthropology, I had learned that personality characteristics are not determined by race, and that it was unscientific to think otherwise! To a card-carrying Nazi, such a statement was, of course, blasphemous and he felt constrained to make a passionate attempt to restore to proper order the chaotic reasoning of my obviously deranged mind. I nodded with great interest, asked him from time to time to clarify some details, and generally managed to feign such fascination with his discourse, that he drivelled on and on. This pleased me greatly, as I was much happier with his lecture than with his questions!

During this riveting sermon an SS-officer came into the room looking for something. When he passed me, he suddenly stopped and looked at me carefully. At the time I happened to have a rather unfortunate facial rash, which made me more noticeable than I could wish, and that not only for security reasons. My heart missed a beat when the SS-er bluntly asked me if he could possibly have seen me recently on the train from Brussels to Antwerp! I managed to burst out laughing at this preposterous suggestion, and apparently did so with enough conviction for him to back off, albeit with a puzzled expression on his face.

But I did actually have a flashback of bumping into the man in the corridor of that train, and politely mumbling: *"Verzeihung"* (Excuse me). I had not recognised him at once because now he was in uniform. But even today I am still filled with admiration for the keen eye of this obviously very professional German policeman!

When, some time later, my interrogator had finished his sermon on the indisputable veracity of national-socialist ideology and its inherent sacred duty to purify the superior Aryan race from any corruption of Jewish blood, I thanked him for having given me a great deal to think about, and for his brilliant discourse on the philosophy of national-socialism! He smiled conceitedly, which made me bold enough to try and take my leave. This move, unfortunately, made the SD-officer come down to earth and tell me curtly that he had not finished with me yet and that I would remain in custody until he had been able to verify my statements.

I was taken to Weteringschans detention centre and locked in a cell where I joined two elderly men who were as reticent about the reasons for their detention as I was about mine. I first had to make sure that neither of them was an *agent provocateur*, as the Nazis liked to plant informers with suspect detainees. But, from their reactions to the news I could tell them about the developments in the war, and their concern of what could happen to them and their families, I was soon satisfied that they were genuine and above board, and I began to explore the possibilities of escape.

A loose screw in the table gave me the first hint of an – all be it very naive – idea. On the assumption that the bars in front of the window would prove to be hollow, and that I could somehow manage to cut onedeep enough to be able to bend it with the aid of a towel tourniquet, I should be able to get my head and shoulders through. From then on, all I had to do was land on my feet! But problem number one was to get myself a hacksaw. The small barred high-up window of our cell, was hinged and set with panes of wired glass. During the blackout this had to be covered with a detachable contraption consisting of a piece of soft-board fixed onto a wooden frame by means of iron straps. It was not difficult to detach a 4 inch piece of one of these straps. Using the cut in the screw head as a clipper-blade, I then managed to make small teeth on one side of the piece of iron strap, thus making a rudimentary saw small enough to fit into the palm of my hand. With the sharp end of this I then carefully loosened the putty around one of the window panes so that I could lift the pane out of its frame and get to a bar with my makeshift saw, and still be able to replace it quickly when danger approached.

It was, of course, a ludicrous plan but at least it gave me a sense of purpose to actually do something to beat the forced passivity of being locked up, and to keep my sanity. My cell mates watched my efforts wide-eyed, silently shaking their heads at my incredible naivety, but did not try to stop me. I spent the next few nights laboriously filing away at the iron bar with my little handsaw, and it soon became evident that it would take me many weeks to get the job done. And yet I stubbornly kept going, remembering the words of William the Silent: *"N'est besoin d'espérer pour entreprendre, ni de réussir pour persévérer"* (One does not need hope to act, nor success to persevere).

But then, unfortunately, while the three of us were being aired, the guards inspected our cell and discovered the loose pane. When we returned, a couple of burly guards were waiting for us, casually swinging their batons, demanding to know who the devil had had the impudence to damage government property. We just gave them a blank look and shrugged our shoulders. They then said, none too tenderly, that a good beating would get the truth out of at least one of us! My sterling cellmates just stared at them silently, but as I hated the thought that these innocent elderly men would be my scapegoats, I stepped forward and told them I was the culprit.

The guards then took me straight to the office of the Governor, who turned out to be a tiny, distinctly Asian-looking, probably Japanese SS-officer. He sat enthroned behind a vastly oversized desk and looked at me with abject distaste through his thick gold-rimmed glasses. At first he merely listened to the report of my wrongdoings with an expression of utter contempt. But when the guards mentioned that, during the inspection of my cell, the offending windowpane had fallen out of its frame and shattered, he angrily jumped to his feet. Turning puce and growling like a tiger, he menacingly came at me from behind his desk and began to shout abuse in a kind of pidgin German. Because of his runtish stature the effect was rather more ludicrous than threatening and I could not suppress a smile. This obviously got his goat, and he snarled at me, stepped forward, reached up on tiptoe and slapped me in the face.

I was so stunned by this sudden physical attack, which I had not expected and least of all coming from an Asian and one of his size, that, instead of retreating, I stumbled forward and slightly bumped into him, making him loose his balance. "Yellow" with fear, he whipped back behind the safety of his huge desk and, fumbling at the holster of his

Luger, he shouted in a falsetto voice: *"Hinaus mit ihm! Sofort! Schnell! Schnell!"* (Out with him! At once! Hurry).

The frightened guards pushed me out of the office and threw me into an isolation cell where I was chained at both hands and feet. I was now not only a despicable jailbreaker, but also a dangerous terrorist who had had the nerve to threaten the Governor! This act of brutality had to be punished with *Sonderbehandlung* (special treatment)!

My new environment could hardly be called an improvement. There was no furniture at all in the cell, and the only illumination came from a skylight more than 3 meters up. Twice a day they brought me a bucket that I could use for no more than 10 minutes, under close watch No doubt to minimise the need for its use, food and drink were rationed as strictly. Altogether, great hospitality! The prospects were gloomy, as I had no idea how long they would keep me there. I certainly seemed to have well and truly messed up my chances of early release.

On the third day, I was unexpectedly handcuffed and taken to Euterpestraat where three SD agents were waiting to interrogate me. One of them greeted me with a nasty grin and the cheery message:

"Jetzt wissen wir aber wer Sie sind, Herr Pelser!" (Now we know who you really are, Mr. Pelser). He then told me smugly that they had heard from Dries how I had helped Jews to escape to Switzerland, and so committed a serious offence against German regulations.

I calmly denied everything, and said that it was clearly a fairy tale they had been telling me, that I had never heard of this Ekker-person, and would love to meet this stranger who was spreading such malicious rumours about me. They then showed me Dries's photo on his fake I.D. card, whereupon I shrugged my shoulders and told them, without batting an eye, that I had never seen this man before. They yelled and screamed and threatened me but, although I was handcuffed, they never laid a finger on me. Perhaps because of my reputation as a notoriously dangerous terrorist? I shall never know. However, as I did not give an inch, they eventually sent me back to my isolation cell, growling that I had not seen the last of them.

A few days later I was again taken from my cell. This time they took me back to the office of the Governor who was conspicuous by his absence. I was ordered to stand with my face to the wall. A little later I heard someone being brought in, and I was told to turn around. To my great surprise I was standing face to face with my old buddy Dries!

Obviously the SD had thought to get my confession by putting us face to face! Dries describes what happened next:

After a few days they took me back to Euterpestraat for interrogations. I had, in the meantime, taken stock of what I could be charged with: journeys to Belgium, without a doubt; to France, probably; but Switzerland? Nobody knew that I had been there! Van Poppel knew about Pelser's first attempt to get there, but because it had failed the S.D. would probably not pay too much attention to a report from an agent of the Abwehr, their arch rivals. And then there was the small matter of the deeds our previously captured friends had credited us with, always supposing that we were safe and sound in Switzerland . . .

Each time we set out on a journey, Pelser and I had kept to our fixed routine and made up a detailed tale to spin the Germans in case we were caught, so that we would always be able to back each other up. This way, we would always have the same story of how we had been helped by a host of – fictitious but meticulously described – men and women, of whom we sadly could not provide addresses as we had only ever seen them at pre-arranged rendez-vous. Unfortunately, our concoctions had become numerous and, to make matters worse, we had never thought up a story to cover the time we spent in The Netherlands.

In the days and nights that passed before my next interrogation I was able to order my thoughts. On the assumption that the S.D. knew about our journeys in France, but was not aware that we had actually been in Switzerland, I took the old stories and cobbled together a new one, naming a lot of contacts who could not be traced because they either simply did not exist or because they had safely gone underground a long time ago.

I assumed the demeanour of a dejected and most contrite miscreant and spent hour upon hour disgorging my part truth, part fairy tale to a not overly bright Sachbearbeiter (an official in charge of preparing the case), who was obviously deeply impressed by what he was hearing. As the words came gushing out in a seemingly endless stream, he must have been convinced that I really wanted to make a clean breast of it. Furthermore, he did not seem to know as much about me as I had feared and he probably thought I was the catch of a lifetime.

He showed great sympathy and passed me his full pack of cigarettes, from which I helped myself greedily, stubbing out each successive cigarette after three puffs and saving that fag-end in a hidden pocket for my cell mates. Why the hell did I do all these stupid things, he pondered. Awful, what problems at home can do to a man! "Nah ja, ach Herr Ekker, der Kopt wird nicht fallen . . . !' (Well, don't worry, Mr. Ekker, you won't hang for this . . .) was his comment.

When I was left in peace and not questioned for several days, I became quite worried. I had made contact with Van Stokkum through a central heating duct, but neither of us knew whether Pelser had been arrested. But then, on a Saturday morning, I was taken to the Warden's office, where I found Pelser standing facing the wall. Behind me were three SD agents who ordered him to turn and face me. It appeared that they had not been able to get a single word out of him. Hence the confrontation: "Nah, Herr Ekker, erzählen Sie jetzt mal was Sie uns erzählt haben" (Well, Mr. Ekker, why don't you tell him what you have told us).

And so I was able to repeat the exact story I had given my interrogators, all the while standing in front of three SD agents who did not see the signs and signals I was giving Pelser because they were assiduously watching him but not me! From then on we were able to back each other up and dovetail our confessions exactly.

Following this confrontation, I could safely play out the role of a penitent sinner, who was greatly relieved by the opportunity to unburden his soul!

SOLITARY CONFINEMENT IN SCHEVENINGEN

The next day I was transferred to the *Oranje Hotel* (the popular epithet of the prison in Scheveningen where most resistance activists were locked up), where I was put into *Einzelhaft* (solitary confinement) in cell 704 on "F" floor. There the notorious *Wachtmeister* (sergeant) Weicke ruled the roost, an SS-er, who welcomed me with an unpleasant smile and the ominous words: *"Wieder einmal so ein verdammter Judenfreund!"* (Another damned Jew lover). I was soon to know exactly how much sympathy he had for us! A few days later he suddenly flung open the door of my cell and barked at me: *"auf Termin"* which meant that first I had to stand to attention in the corridor with my nose touching the wall for about an hour and was then taken away to be interrogated at the SD headquarters somewhere in The Hague.

My *Sachbearbeiter,* (the official in charge of my case) a certain Herr Bauer, was a professional policeman of whom I never got the impression that he was a fervent devotee of Nazi ideology. It soon turned out that he had also interrogated Dries. Herr Bauer was far from stupid but apparently had his reasons to gloss over any possible discrepancies between our statements, and clearly took great pains to make sure our confessions matched. He hardly ever raised his voice, but took his time and, when I was not quite sure or had missed a detail of the story, usually reminded me tactfully of what Dries had said at that point. He did his best to create a relaxed atmosphere and was most generous with his cigarettes. But I stayed on the alert for any possible trap.

Only once did he ask me casually whether I knew Jan Meijer, but when I offhandedly said that I had never even heard the name, he did not pursue the question any further. My possible involvement with *Het Parool* never came up again, which could only mean that Jan Meijer and Wim van Norden had managed to keep their mouths shut about me.

Meanwhile, I had to try and cope as best I could with my solitary confinement. In retrospect, I think that it took me about four months to fully take hold of myself again, and it was far from easy. I had never realised how difficult it is to be totally cut off from decent human contact and I could never look at the occasional bird that came to rest on my windowsill without being acutely envious of its freedom to fly away. At first I could not help worrying about what was in store for me. I seriously considered the possibility that I might get the death penalty for espionage and be shot. I even used my anatomical knowledge to calculate the chances of surviving the firing squad! Then one day I found on the cart of the prison library that came round once a week, a manual on infinitesimal calculus in French. I also acquired a slate and pencil, so that I could practice the exercises in the book. From then on I immersed myself in this abstract world which stopped me thinking about reality and worrying about my own situation and that of my loved ones. Slowly but surely my equilibrium was restored.

After the war, when I read Koestler's *Darkness at Noon*, I recognised my experience in his description of the way in which political prisoners in the Soviet Union kept their sanity by playing blind games of chess!

Coping with the never ending harassment by Wachtmeister Weicke was another matter. I soon found that he took a malicious pleasure in dishing out *kalte Kost* (cold food) for one or more days to punish even the slightest infraction of the Spartan regime he reserved for his favourite victims. At first I thought that this punishment would only mean not getting a hot meal, but it actually meant getting no food at all! For a *Judenfreund* like me, there was a special set of rules that had to be obeyed to the letter:

a) whenever Weicke would walk into the cell, the prisoner was to promptly snap to attention at a set place in front of the bed and recite, with feeling: *"Haftling Nummer sechs-hundert-funfzehn, anwesend!"* (prisoner number 615, present!);

b) at reveille the prisoner was to get up promptly and immediately start to fold his blankets into a neat rectangular with trimly squared sides which Weicke would occasionally run his finger over to check for any irregularities;

c) the cell was to be kept meticulously clean of any dust, straw, crumbs of bread, grains of sugar, or any other "dirt" that might offend His Excellency's sensibilities. He once made me scrub the floor of my cell with my toothbrush over and over again because *"ein schmutziges Judenschwein"* (a dirty pig of a Jew) like me should be taught some Aryan cleanliness!

The Spartan regime also meant that prisoners in solitary confinement could not go to the barber. This way I found out that I look absolutely ridiculous in a moustache as it turns out that one side of my upper lip produces red hair, while the other grows blond, resulting in a decidedly clownish appearance! Anyway, after a few weeks, I had sprouted quite an impressive if unruly beard. I found it scratchy and uncomfortable, and would have loved to be rid of it, but had little choice in the matter. One propitious day, however, disaster galloped to the rescue! Deeply absorbed in my mathematical exercises, I absentmindedly scratched my head and noticed something dropping onto the page in front of me. Upon closer investigation, I had to come to the uncomfortable conclusion that, on the assumption that my time spent in parasitology had not been entirely wasted, the creature wriggling on my book was a pediculus capitis or common head louse! Just to make sure, I passed a comb through my hair and was horrified to see that a whole colony of the little buggers rained down on the pages of my book.

I alerted Weicke and, standing to exemplary attention, told him that I had inadvertently acquired some lodgers. He looked at me with disgust, hastily exited my cell into the corridor and shouted *"Heraus! Los, los, Gesicht an der Wand!"* (Out, hurry up, face to the wall!). He left me there and returned, a little later, with a cleaning detail that he instructed to clear out and burn the contents to my cell. I was then marched off to the barber where I got my head shaved and anointed with a rather foul smelling and stinging lotion. I was told to bathe and given a clean set of prison clothes whereupon I returned to my quarters, smelling rather horribly of creosote but feeling human again and very grateful to the tiny parasite that had earned me the luxury of a hot shower!

Unfortunately, my cleanshaven exterior did nothing to endear me to Wachtmeister Weicke. At first his deliberate humiliations continued to anger me but, as I realised that defiance could only result in more severe harassment or worse, I decided to keep a stiff upper lip. And when I had learned the hard way that challenging the rules would only endanger my food supply, I made an effort to show my malicious tormentor that even a despised *Judenfreund* could behave like a model prisoner.

What I did not realise at the time, however, was that the enforced suppression of emotions and my calculated efforts to please my sadistic jailer gradually led to an unfortunate deviation from my normal behaviour. When, after about two months, my solitary confinement was lifted, I did not really feel like communicating with my cellmates anymore. This was not so much out of fear for an informer, but – as I realised only much later – mainly because I often felt contempt for their anxieties, especially in view of the often petty reasons for their confinement. Many of them were just black marketeers or common thieves or people who had been found not to have handed in their copperware as the Nazis had ordered, or who had been accused of listening to the BBC. When asked, all of them would say that they hated the Germans, but it would not even occur to any of them to risk his neck and join the Resistance.

One time, a student of Egyptology was brought in because the SD had found subversive pamphlets in his room. I tried a few times to talk with him about the subject of his studies, which had always interested me, but as he was totally convinced that he would get the bullet, he would not even listen to me. I tried hard not to show my contempt for this pathetic excuse of a man, but he really stretched my patience when, having been told that he would be released the next morning, he had the gall to gobble up a whole pound of sugar, a whole month's ration which had been issued that very day, instead of leaving it behind for his hungry cell mates! So I did not make the slightest attempt to contain my mirth when, as a result of his appalling greed, he had a serious attack of the runs throughout that night!

A more serious sign of my changed mental disposition, however, became obvious when, some time later, an equally panicked prisoner was put in our cell.

This man had every reason to be terrified: not only had he been caught red-handed as a gun-carrying saboteur but he was a Jew to boot! Quite enough for the Nazis to have him summarily executed which, shortly afterwards, they did.

No wonder that he was literally sweating with fear and, amongst strangers whom he naturally did not trust, most uncommunicative. Although I deeply sympathised with him, he nevertheless really irritated me, for no apparent reason at all. Even today, I still do not know why. Was it his silent, but almost tangible reproach for our incapacity to understand what he was going through? Was it because he reminded me of what could happen to my Jewish girlfriend and her family who, for various reasons, I had not been able to save from the clutches of the Nazis? Or was it because he confronted me with a situation that I too might possibly have to face one day? Anyhow, I could not help but stare at him constantly. He was a tall, nice looking, strongly built fellow with an open face and the callused hands of a manual labourer, quite the opposite, in fact, of how the Nazi propaganda machine used to paint the typical Jew. Why the hell then could he not manage to be more dignified and composed?! After a while, strangely enough, my irritation fixed on a few black hairs sprouting from the knob of his nose. I could not keep my eyes from them, as if this conspicuous disfigurement (remember my own facial rash!) were the cause of his undignified behaviour! Then, quite inadvertently, something he said or did – I cannot remember what it was – made me jump to my feet in a fit of anger and, most uncharacteristically, I punched him on the nose!

He just shoved me aside and gave me a look which I still cannot forget and I still feel the shame and humiliation, which swept me when I realised what I had done. There I was, awkwardly stammering an apology, and he just looked at me, making it bloody obvious how right he had been never to trust a Gentile! The very next day he was transferred, no doubt to meet his fate. I never had the chance to make up for my outrageous behaviour, which has had an impact on me for the rest of my life!

When, many years later, I became more knowledgeable about the psychology of victims of persecution and tyranny, I found a possible explanation for my deviant behaviour. I learned that people who are starving and in constant fear of their life and who also are subjected to humiliation through verbal and physical abuse, often suffer from a kind of depersonalisation. In this condition "normal" standards of civilised behaviour and morals seem to decline and are replaced by a self-centred and antisocial set of rules, wholly aimed at survival and self-preservation. Some psychiatrists developed the theory that a certain psychological mechanism: the identification with the powerful oppressor, is at the root of this aberrant behaviour. This mechanism should explain why, in these conditions, reasonable and "normal" individuals can turn into inhuman brutes who, when given the power, seem to enjoy mistreating and torturing their fellow-prisoners more zealously than the oppressor would do himself. In retrospect I have often wondered whether during my detention under Wachtmeister Weicke I somehow had become subject to this mechanism myself.

In March 1944, while I was standing in the corridor waiting to be transferred for trial to Utrecht, I saw Wachtmeister Weicke making his rounds. It suddenly occurred to me that I now had a chance to take subtle revenge for what this man had made me suffer. When he passed me, I jumped to attention and said: *"Bitte Herr Wachtmeister, ich möchte mich von Ihnen verabschieden"* (Excuse me sir, I would like to say goodbye). He stopped and looked at me as if he could not believe his ears. I went on: *"Ich möchte mich gefälligst bei Ihnen bedanken für das Viele was ich von Ihnen gelernt habe."* (I should like to thank you very much for all you have taught me.) His jaw dropped and, for a moment, he stared at me pop-eyed and then, without a word, he continued his rounds.

Enjoying my sweet revenge, I could not help but chuckle at his obvious confusion over the courteous good-bye of a damned *Judenfreund*, but lately I have wondered whether, deep down, there was not a streak of the identification mechanism at work, which caused me to do what I did.

GERMAN JUSTICE

Anyway, a little later I met my good buddy Dries again, whom I had not seen for about 10 months. He had not changed at all and was delighted to see me. We were handcuffed to each other and put on the train to Utrecht where our trial was to take place. Our guards spent the trip busily chatting with each other, and we did the same, catching up on the past year's events.

In Utrecht, while we were escorted from the station to nearby Wolvenplein prison, I noticed that our handcuffs had not been properly locked and that we could have easily got rid of them and made a run for it. It was too late to do that then, but probably just as well as it may well have been a ploy to try and make us escape and have an excuse to shoot us in the back.

A few days later, on March 14th, 1944, Dries and I were tried before the *Deutsche Obergericht* (German High Court) together with Ward Messer and the three *passeurs* from Roosendaal, the Roosenbooms and

Oompje Schoenmakers who, amongst others, had helped the Frenkels to cross the Dutch-Belgian border.

Mathieu Smedts had been compromised by his contacts with a communist activist, Dr. Kastein, who was involved in the liquidation of General Seyffardt, a prominent Dutch Nazi, and with Kees Dutilh who had been operating a sabotage and spying cell, both of whom had been caught in the nets of the traitor Anton van der Waals. Although Mat had been approached by these people, he had never actually been involved with either of them. Nevertheless, he was sentenced to death for espionage by the *Heeresgericht* (military tribunal) on November 17th, 1943. Fortunately, however, the execution was postponed indefinitely and Mathieu was transferred in *Nacht und Nebel* (literally: "into darkness and fog", meaning that officially one ceased to exist) to notorious detention centres in Germany, first Sonnenburg, then Wolfenbüttel, both of which he, mercifully, survived.

As our case had been *abgetrennt* (separated) from the more serious case of Mathieu's, we were only sentenced to ordinary prison terms. Much to our surprise, however, the German High Court President, *Obergerichtspräsident* Herr Joppich, sentenced Dries to 15 months imprisonment, but Ward and me to only 10 months and all of us with remission for time already served. The argument for the difference was that Dries was a rogue who had tried to make money out of the misery of others (the Jews), whereas Ward and I, although we too had violated German regulations – which, of course, could not be tolerated and had to be punished – had been motivated by feelings of compassion towards our friends, which did not make it right, but it was at least humanly understandable! From a Nazi court of justice a most remarkable verdict indeed!

As far as the court knew, the only "crime" Dries and I had committed had been to take people illegally across the Belgian border, and to travel to France without permission. Had they known about my work for *Het Parool* and of our trip to Switzerland, both of us would not have got off so lightly! I had already served 11 months in prison, and Ward even 15. So the two of us were to be released immediately, but as the prison administration office was closed by the time the trial had ended, we could only be discharged the next day.

I hardly slept that night, partly from excitement at the prospect of imminent freedom, but also because I was busy memorising messages from my cell mates, which I was to deliver to their relatives.

VII

"...OUTRAGEOUS FORTUNE..."

PRISONER OF WAR

The next morning, however, after I had hurriedly completed the discharge forms, I was way-laid at the prison-gate by two Dutch military policemen who told me that they had orders to take me to the military reception camp for POWs in Amersfoort! I was shocked and outraged, but what could I do? Only a little later I came to know that this nasty trick had been played on me by the SD. It was a political decision not to let me go, exacerbated by the fact that their rival, the *Abwehr* (German Counter-espionage Service), was particularly keen to turn me loose and use me as bait to catch bigger fish.

On my arrival in the Amersfoort POW camp, I immediately demanded to see the Commanding Officer. He was an elderly *Wehrmacht* officer, who received me correctly and asked me what I wanted. I told him that I had served in the Army Medical Corps and could not be taken POW under the Geneva Convention. Therefore he had no right to send me to a POW camp. Obviously embarrassed, he said: *"Aber Herr Pelser, Sie wissen doch was gegen Ihnen vorliegt!"* (But Mr. Pelser, you surely must know what they are holding against you.) I protested that I had been tried by a German court of justice, and had more than fully paid my dues. He turned his eyes away and said: *"Es tut mir leid, Herr Pelser, aber da Sie der Sicherheitsdienst nach deutschfeindlich sind, gehen Sie entweder freiwillig in Kriegsgefangenschaft, oder Sie verschwinden in Nacht und Nebel.*" (I am sorry, Mr. Pelser, but as the Security Service considers you to be an enemy of the German Reich, you either agree to go to a POW camp, or nobody will ever hear of you again.) He could not have put it more clearly and I had little option but to agree to the first choice.

Friends of mine in Amsterdam brought me my uniform and what was left of my military kit, and some days later I and some other unfortunates were on our way to Stalag 4-B (short for *Stammlager* or base camp) in Mühlberg an der Elbe, Germany.

We travelled in a freight train, which was far from comfortable but the food was just edible and the journey only took three days, so we did not grumble too much. Three of my fellow-passengers actually were great fun. One was Mr. 's Jacob, the Mayor of a small town in Gelderland, who had been dismissed for his rather lackadaisical attitude to German regulations. Another one was Dr. Erkelens, a medical reserve officer, sent to Mühlberg as relief, and the third was Van Gelder, a reserve officer cadet, who had tried to escape POW camp by going into hiding but had had the bad luck to be caught in a *razzia*.

When we arrived in Mühlberg, we were temporarily put up in a barracks outside the camp. According to the *Transportführer* (transport officer) I was supposed to be transferred to some place near Stuttgart. Although 's Jacob and Van Gelder were soon moved to an officers' POW camp, and Dr. Erkelens went to the hospital, nobody seemed to know quite what to do with me, as it turned out that the Transportführer had lost my file! So I was left to my own devices with nothing to do but an occasional game of chess with the guards who were equally bored.

One of them, a history student, was my age. As he turned out to be a convinced Nazi, I thoroughly enjoyed goading him with discussions on the ideology of Naziism. He actually knew his classics fairly well and quoted ad lib from Plato, Hegel and Schopenhauer. But it was not too difficult to corner him philosophically on the absurdity of Alfred Rosenberg's *"Rassenlehre"* (racial theory) or the ludicrous concept of the Arische Übermensch (Aryan superman). I took great pleasure in teasing him with the scientific and cultural contributions of geniuses like Einstein, Spinoza, Maimonides, Adler or Freud, and artists like Mendelssohn, Chagall, Thomas Mann or Stephan Zweig, all of them Jews. This obviously irritated him intensely, but as he was clever enough to acknowledge my points, he tried to belittle them as *Beispiele einer altmodisch bürgerlichen fehlgeleiteten Denkart* (examples of a thought process that was old-fashioned, bourgeois and steeped in error), which only caused me to laugh in his face.

At last I was taken to the Camp Commandant, a dapper, quite short, elderly *Wehrmacht* colonel who himself had been a POW of the Russians in WW.I. He sported a martial moustache and had a beetle brow from under which he looked at me in my shabby uniform with a mixture of puzzlement and contempt. He wanted to know what the emblem on my collar stood for. I explained that it was a wreath of laurels around an Aesculapian staff, showing that I was a medical officer cadet. *"Sind Sie Arzt?"* (are you a qualified doctor) he asked me. *"Nein, Herr Oberst, ich bin noch kein Arzt, aber trotzdem weiss ich mehr von Medizin als viele deutsche Ärzte"* (no Sir, I am not yet qualified, but I still know more about medicine than many German doctors), I replied with appropriate modesty. His reaction was most satisfying: he yelped as though stung by a wasp, turned purple in the face and screamed: *"Unverschämter Hund, was bilden Sie sich ein!"* (Impertinent dog, who do you think you are!). When I made no move to apologise, he shouted: *"Hinaus! Ich werde mich persönlich dafür einsetzen dass Sie hier niemals ärztlich tätig sein werden!"* (Out! I will personally see to it that you will never practice medicine in this place!), and ordered me to be assigned to the infirmary as a laboratory technician and to be accommodated with the orderlies, rather than with the doctors, which suited me just fine.

I soon made friends with the other laboratory technician, Danilo Perandini, an Italian medical student who had been taken POW when he and his unit had refused to fight on the side of the Nazis any longer after General Badoglio had switched over to the Allied side in September 1943. Danilo's father had been a very good friend of the famous Italian socialist and trade-union leader Matteotti who was murdered by the Fascists in 1924, and consequently Danilo had been brought up with a healthy dislike for Mussolini and his lot. But he also despised the Italian army and especially its officers whom he blamed for the deaths of thousands of Italian soldiers, massacred by the *Waffen-SS* in reprisal for Badoglio's capitulation to the Allies.

Later, Danilo introduced me to a friend of his who had actually survived the massacre that took place on the Greek islet of Cephalonia where the SS butchered the whole Italian garrison of more than 5000 to the last man. This soldier was amongst them, but happened not to be fatally hit by the machine-gun fire. He dropped down amongst his comrades and, covered with their blood, feigned to be dead. An SS-officer went round to finish off anyone still moving and stood near him for what seemed like an eternity. He held his breath, but the officer nevertheless gave him a neck shot. He passed out, but the bullet had actually passed straight through his throat without causing any damage to the great vessels and he miraculously lived. When he regained consciousness it was night. He crawled out from under the corpses and staggered to a nearby Greek village, where he was taken in and lovingly nursed back to health. Seeing the scars on both sides of his neck rekindled the fantasies I had had about surviving a firing squad when I still expected to face one myself! Here, before my very eyes. I had the proof that it was possible!

Danilo was a nice fellow. He was usually very kind to the patients sent to the laboratory to have a blood sample taken or a sample of their gastric juice. As we had no proper equipment, we had to collect the latter with a thick rubber tube inserted through the patient's mouth.

The only patients who Danilo could not stand, were the, usually Yugoslav, POWs who did not, or feigned not to, understand explanations or instructions given in any civilised language and just sat there with bulging eyes and their mouths tightly shut. But Danilo and I soon found out how we could get the job done quickly and efficiently: we stood on either side of the frightened patient, one of us holding the receptacle for the gastric juice and the other keeping the tube carefully out of sight. On a signal the former trod hard on the toes of the hapless patient who unfailingly jumped up with a shout. The other then quickly inserted the tube through the suddenly wide-open mouth with one hand while, with the other, he pushed the victim down in his seat so firmly that the pressure in the patient's stomach was enough for a blob of gastric juice to come up through the tube. It really was a piece of cake and, with practice, took us no more than half a minute.

Another fascinating person in the hospital was our headnurse, Herman Hammelburg, an Amsterdam Jew who was, in fact, hiding in our camp as a registered POW in order to escape Nazi persecution. When the Nazis had started large scale *razzias* on Jewish people in Amsterdam, he had bought a second hand sergeant's uniform, and reported himself as a POW, using the military identification of his, already deported, brother. By means of this simple but clever trick, he managed to escape deportation to one of the Nazi death camps and survived the war. He was a nice, intelligent fellow and an excellent nurse. A few years after the war he went to Israel where he studied physiotherapy, and eventually became Director of a revalidation centre.

Herman used his position as headnurse to guard our radio, which had been secretly designed and assembled to fit into a microscope case by a fellow POW, a professional radio operator. We listened daily to the BBC news and kept track of the front lines on a map in the doctor's room, which was so up to date that many Germans used to sneak in for a look. As they themselves only got the news from their notoriously unreliable propaganda broadcasts, they were totally at a loss as to how on earth we got our information so quickly and accurately. Whenever the routine search for secret radio sets took place during the day, the set was in the microscope case in the laboratory. The Germans did not much care to come there because Danilo and I made a point of telling them, at appropriate intervals, how dangerously infectious the material was that we were working with. But, if unexpectedly they should make a search during the night, the laboratory would be unattended and they might well find the radio by chance. Hammelburg, as headnurse, was responsible for all medical equipment. At the end of each day he would take the microscope case, with the radio set locked inside, to the Administration office, to put this so very precious instrument into the safekeeping of the German Bureau Chief himself. The thick-headed Germans never knew that the radio they were so assiduously hunting was right under their noses most of the time!

But the true extent of their stupidity only became apparent some time later. In the absence of cameras, my ability to draw true-to-life portraits made me many friends, in particular amongst the nursing staff of the "Desert Rats", who had been captured at Tobrouk as early as June 1942. When I wondered why they had never been exchanged and sent home which, as medical personnel, they were entitled to under the Geneva Convention, they told me that this was only possible with an official RAMC stamp in their papers. As nobody in England ever considered the possibility of capture, most of them had never bothered to get such a stamp. I told them that if they could get me an authentic sample, I could try and reproduce it. Eventually they managed to get one. It was fun to be able to turn my hand to a nice bit of forgery again! I copied the original stamp with an aniline pencil and, with a pointed matchstick and some spittle, blurred the lines to make them look exactly like the impression of a rubber stamp. The happy owner sent his newly embellished service record booklet to the German administration to be registered and duly got it back *"zum Austausch genehmigt"* (approved for exchange)!

The news of this success spread quickly and soon I received many more such commissions. It seemed only prudent to make sure that the forgeries were not identical, and therefore I requested a larger variety of samples. The Germans o.k.'d each one of my masterpieces, bar the time when they found a stamp with a date which had expired. I brazenly added a stamp from a model that had been accepted before. The papers were submitted again and, much to our surprise, returned "Approved". The Germans obviously never noticed that apparently the same issuing office had stamped the papers twice but on separate dates. So much for official Nazi bureaucracy! I did not know that the war would end before my clients could cash in their newly forged return tickets and it never really spoiled the fun of having had one over on the Germans once again.

The Russians were the only POWs we never saw at the laboratory. As the Soviet Union had not signed the Geneva Convention, the Russian POWs were completely at the mercy of the Nazis. Soviet prisoners were kept in a separate barbed-wire enclosure within the POW camp and starved, much like the political prisoners of the Nazis. They also were denied medical assistance or access to the Red Cross. In Mühlberg the Russian medics could do a little more than usual for their people. The Camp Commandant, an ex-POW himself, used to turn a blind eye as long as they provided only basic medical care and did not use any of the supplies that were strictly reserved for "regular" POWs.

One of the Russian medics, a Ukrainian called Constantin, regularly brought material to the laboratory for examination. He was a nice chap who spoke French and German fairly well, and was also an excellent chess player. He would sometimes tell us about patients he could not treat properly for lack of medication, and on appeal to either the Dutch doctor or Hammelburg, I usually could give him what he needed, albeit in strictest secrecy. In return, he once smuggled me, disguised as a Russian prisoner, into their compound, to watch one of their traditional amateur theatricals. Although, of course, I could not understand a word of what was said and my friend was too caught up in the play to keep on interpreting for me, the exuberant gestures and mimics of the actors made up for a lot.

Yet I very much preferred the plays which were occasionally put on by the British, not only because I could understand the dialogue, but also because they had a remarkably talented actor who was such a brilliantly sexy transvestite that at each performance the audience fell passionately in love with "her" and had to be forcibly held back from storming the stage in an attempt to assault her! These performances were, needless to say, massively attended, also by the German guards.

Meanwhile, outside, the war was going on. The BBC reports about the D-day invasion and the Allied progress caused great enthusiasm and optimism amongst us, whereas the faces of the Nazis dropped more and more. But, to the Germans, by far the greater fear was caused by the danger from the east and with each advance of the Red Army our guards became a little more co-operative.

This made it easier for me to work on a plan to try and get to the Bergen-Belsen concentration camp near Hannover, where I knew my girlfriend and her family to be. I had calculated that to get from Mühlberg to Hannover would take me about a fortnight and that it would take the British army the same amount of time to get there from the Rhine. To get out of the camp in Mühlberg was not a big deal, but to travel on the stage of the *Götterdämmerung* without a legitimate I.D. might prove to be difficult. Not wanting to open up a can of worms, I carefully chose the dumbest German in the camp office and casually asked him about the risks of I.D. checks on the German roads. His information was far from reassuring. He stressed that all over the country the military police was constantly patrolling and looking for deserters. Only military personnel in uniform, carrying official orders, could get through. My first job therefore, was to find out what official orders looked like.

One day I heard that some POWs had to be escorted to Dresden for examination in a specialist clinic. Using the excuse that, as an artist, I should see the architectural splendours of this beautiful city, I managed to get picked as an assistant escort for this trip. I then claimed that, to see the sights properly, I should be able to move around freely in Dresden, whereupon the fools actually gave me official orders which, of course, I never returned. As I now knew in which drawer these forms were kept, I soon acquired a blank one, which only needed me to copy the stamp and the signature of the Commandant. Thus I was prepared for my journey to Bergen-Belsen and only needed to wait for the British army to cross the Rhine.

Unfortunately, the Allied Forces in the West made slower progress than we had hoped, but when on September 17th the British Airborns launched a massive offensive near Arnhem to capture the bridge across the Rhine, I started to get ready for my trip. When Operation Market Garden sadly turned into a failure, however, I had to postpone my escape.

Meanwhile, the Soviet armies were getting closer. In the first week of October 1944, some Polish women were brought as POWs into our camp. They were put in a separate compound, and we were sent there to look after the sick and wounded.

It was the very first time I saw female combatants. They were indeed a sorry lot! In makeshift uniforms or badly worn civilian clothes, they huddled together, embittered and defeated. They told us that when the Red Army had taken Praga, a suburb of Warsaw on the east-bank of the Weichsel, the underground Polish nationalist army started a revolt against the Germans to try and liberate Warsaw before the Soviets could. Their leader, the General Bor, had counted on the Russians to come to his aid. But the Red Army, probably for political reasons, never moved and, after two months of bitter fighting and heavy casualties, General Bor had to capitulate to the Germans in exchange for an honourable retreat. As usual, however, the Nazis did not keep their word and took them all prisoner, but otherwise did not treat them too badly.

One of these girls was a medical student. As she was the first pretty woman I had seen in many years, and she spoke French fluently, I enjoyed talking to her. But she suffered from a bad cough and was running a fever which made me think that she might have pneumonia. I gave her some sulfanilamid tablets, but was unable to see the result as she and her comrades were transferred the very next day. Many years after the war, however, when the communist rule in her country had crumbled, she sent me a letter to thank me for having saved her life and to tell me that she still lived in her hometown, Poznan, and had become a physician, just like me.

On Christmas Eve 1944, we were suddenly called to unload a few trucks carrying American POWs, captured during the German offensive in the Ardennes. Most of these unfortunate chaps were greenhorns, flown over from New York to the frontline only days before the German division had launched its attack. They had been on the move for about a week, without any food or drink, in freezing weather and in unheated freight carriages! Some of them had literally frozen to death, many were suffering from pneumonia and the rest was actually too weak to stand on their feet. We rushed them to the hospital, which could only take the worse cases. The dead were put in a separate room. When we had finished, I went back there and checked, just to make sure, if by any chance somebody might still be alive. In one of the supposed corpses I actually found a barely audible heartbeat. I carried the body into the ward for further examination. Major Ochse, a South African physician who was on duty, shook his head in disbelief but when, on percussion, he found massive dullness over both lungs, he decided to give the man the benefit of the doubt and injected him with a large dose of the new drug which the American medics carried with them: penicillin.

The next day I simply could not believe my eyes when I saw last night's corpse sitting up in his bunk and stuffing his face with porridge as though it was the most delicious food he had ever tasted. To my astonishment he and all the other patients with pneumonia made a full recovery in less than a week. It was my first experience of the life saving potential of this wonder drug and I realised that what I had seen, was a revolutionary advance in the treatment of bacterial infections.

Meanwhile, we had to cope with the unpleasant effects of a bitterly cold winter. Due to the serious damage done to the German railway network by Allied bombs, we had to put up with an increasing lack of fuel and a rapidly deteriorating food situation. Our rations of, always stale, sourdough bread became smaller and smaller, and the unsavoury German swede soup more watery.

Life was beginning to get a little uncivilised, especially for the Dutch POWs who, for some mysterious reason, were not supplied with Red Cross parcels. I was lucky in that I had made some nice and hospitable friends amongst the British medics who often treated me to a mug of their wonderful hot, strong brew, some biscuits and a real Virginia cigarette.

Another, rather unfortunate, result of the bitter cold was that all the drains were frozen which meant that the latrines had turned into one giant cesspool so appallingly foul that we tried at all costs to keep well away. In spite of the cold, most of us preferred to find a sheltered spot outside to relieve ourselves. I happened to occupy the top bunk, right next to a window that was always left open at night to provide some very necessary fresh air! To perform my bodily functions with a minimum of discomfort I had perfected an excellent technique that obviated the necessity to leave my warm bed at night: I simply aimed for the open window and peed through it! This worked fine until, one very cold night, I had not noticed that the poor chap sleeping on the bottom bunk had closed the window. In the middle of the night I blithely performed my party trick and was startled when suddenly a cry came up that he was being rained on and could I shut the bloody window! I hastily told him that he must have had a wet dream and to go back to sleep. I thought that, in the circumstances, it was by far the kinder thing to spare him the truth!

On March 7th, 1945, American tanks crossed the Rhine at Remagen, and soon were pushing in our direction. As a result, German military vigilance in our area increased so much that I had to reconsider my plan to get to Bergen-Belsen, despite the fact that the British army crossed the Rhine near Wesel only two weeks later. I decided to wait and see how things were going and that eventually turned out to be a very happy decision.

In the night of April 22nd, 1945, the rapid approach of the Soviets apparently became too much for our heroic German guards and, under cover of darkness, they abandoned their posts and fled Westward to give themselves up to the Americans.

LIBERATION

On April 23rd, 1945, we were not woken by the usual Teutonic clamour hailing the break of a new day but by confused and excited shouts of early risers who had found the watchtowers deserted and the main gate unguarded. We opened the gate and looked around outside to see what was going on, but nobody seemed to know what to do. About 7 a.m. however, three heavily armed, mounted Soviet scouts galloped in and, amidst welcoming cheers from the crowd, rode straight for the Russian compound. There, one of them, obviously their commander, shouted something whereupon some five or six Russian POWs, probably informants of the Germans, were dragged to the wall of the nearest barracks and shot!

The whole thing was over in less than five minutes. The commander then leapt onto a table and made a short speech, at the end of which he pointed to the edge of a wood on a hillside about half a mile east, where some camouflaged vehicles could just be made out amongst the trees, and shouted: "There is the Red Army!" or words to that effect. With a jubilant cry the whole body of Russians, resembling nothing more than a herd of stampeding cattle, then pushed itself, as a man, through the two barbed wire fences, and streamed across the open land between the camp and the hillock, leaving behind many who were trampled to death in the process. A farmhouse and a few barns standing in their way were all on fire and not a single creature was left alive when the last Russian had passed. I never saw a more breathtaking illustration of Ortega Y Gasset's "Revolt of the Hordes"!

Through an interpreter, the commander of the Russian scouts then instructed the senior officers of the other POWs that, because the fighting was still going on, nobody was to leave the camp until the Red Army had taken over, and that food and transport would be provided in due course.

Only two days later the Russians actually reached Torgau, a little town some 20 km north of Mühlberg on the east bank of the Elbe, where the historical meeting with the American First Army took place on April 25th, 1945.

Meanwhile Herman Hammelburg had heard that, not far from our camp, a freight train packed with people was stranded at the spot where, a few days earlier, a munitions train had blown up and destroyed the track. With nobody around to stop him, he organised some form of transport and wandered off there to have a look. He returned with about forty badly emaciated and very ill people, most of whom were suffering from typhus and took them straight to the hospital outside our camp.

When I saw them, I found that they were Dutch Jews from Bergen-Belsen. I tried, of course, to find out if anybody knew anything about my girlfriend and her family.

Unfortunately, these people only told me confused and contradictory stories, as they were too ill to think about anything but their own misery. They only knew that in Bergen-Belsen they had been put on a train, and told that they were to be gassed in Auschwitz. But as the track going east was cut off by the advancing Red Army, the Nazis apparently decided to drive the train into the Elbe and drown the Jews instead. Two days previously, however, the train was suddenly held up by Russian soldiers who had taken the Germans prisoner and told the passengers to go to the nearby village and help themselves – housing, food, clothing, it was all theirs for the taking. A lot of them went, but these patients had been too weak to get off the train. They only knew that they had been collected by somebody who spoke Dutch (Hammelburg) and brought to this place, but they had not the faintest idea where they were or where that train had been stopped.

A little later I heard by chance that patients from the same train had been taken to a sanatorium in Zeithain, only a few miles from our camp. I went there on a bicycle, which the Germans had conveniently left behind. Amongst the patients I found, to my delight, someone I knew quite well, Renate Laqueur, the daughter of my former professor of Pharmacology. Although she had, of course, lost much weight, she remained the pretty girl she always was and in spite of all she had gone through still had her wealth of long and beautifully burnished auburn hair. She told me that the Russians had stopped their train at a place called Tröbitz, and that she had actually seen my girlfriend there foraging for food. When I said good-bye to her, Renate whispered that she had typhus, but had not let on as she was anxious to keep it from the doctors who otherwise would be obliged to shave off her hair. I promised her, of course, to keep my mouth shut, but when the doctor showed me out, he told me, also in strictest confidence, that Renate had not been told that she had typhus as nobody wanted to shave off her beautiful hair! It just goes to show that even a Nazi was sensitive to the charm of a beautiful Jewess.

Meanwhile, although the date for their departure had not yet been fixed, the Dutch POWs were busily preparing to go home. I explained to Bob Potter, the doctor who was now in charge and who had become a good friend of mine, that I did not want to go home before I had found my girlfriend. He agreed, of course, and even gave me his uniform to wear because I was more likely to get through Russian occupied territory as a medical officer of the KNIL (Dutch colonial army) than in the shabby remains of my own uniform. His uniform had been made in Holland quite recently, but because the required green material was not available any more, the tailor had used some of the blue-grey reserved for the Dutch army number one's. The peeked cap that went with the KNIL uniform was made in matching grey. The niceties of the military dress code were totally wasted on me. But it would not be long before I would discover that my notorious lack of interest in social etiquette could have cost me dearly.

So, on May 17th, 1945, I bicycled to Tröbitz, some 24 km from our camp. The only identification document I had was a crumpled piece of paper, written in Russian and bearing the stamp of the Russian commandant in Mühlberg, permitting me to move between the camp and the hospital. I soon found that, even when I was stopped at gunpoint for a check, the Russian soldiers were far more impressed by the stamp than by the text of my pass, which they were often obviously unable to read as they usually held it upside down.

The first thing I saw when I arrived in Tröbitz, was a warning sign in Russian and in German: *"Fleckfieber! Eintritt untersagt!"* (Typhus! No entry!).

I decided this did not apply to me and rode on. I did not see anybody until I came to a square where I saw a few people gathered in a pharmacy. There I happened to find one of my girlfriend's uncles, Dr. Jaap Elte, who was overjoyed to see me. But before we could talk, a couple of Russian soldiers came in, grabbed me and marched me to the *Kommandantura* across the square where I was un-gently shoved inside and put in front of some Russian officers who started to point angrily at my uniform and especially at the cap I was wearing. There was a lot of talk in Russian, which did not sound at all friendly. It might as well have been Sanskrit for all I could understand of it! The only thing that sounded familiar, if not very comforting, was the ominous word "S.S.", and from that and their eloquent gestures, I surmised that they entertained the unpleasant notion of shooting me! Suddenly the penny dropped, and I guessed the reason for their excitement: the cap of my KNIL uniform looked uncannily like the peaked cap of the SS, and the bluish-grey colour of my uniform did nothing to improve on the first impression! I raised my hands in despair and called out in French if there might be someone who could understand *"Franshuski"*. Fortunately one of them, a woman colonel, did. I explained to her that, far from being a member of the SS, I was a Dutch POW as she could tell from the fact that I wore an orange badge on my cap instead of the swastika and skull of the SS. After another rather heated discussion in Russian she told me that they believed me, but ordered me to leave the village immediately, as it was under quarantine because of typhus. I saluted and departed smartly.

Outside, Jaap Elte was waiting for me and took me straight to the house where my girlfriend was living, together with some of her other relatives. Jaap told me that she had been very ill with typhus and had only come out of coma that very morning. He therefore wanted to go and break it to her gently that I had come to see her. He went upstairs and I heard him tell her that he had a big surprise for her, whereupon she immediately said: "Henk is here!", as though it was the most natural thing in the world and she had been expecting me!

She was still in bed, exhausted from lack of food and high fever, but seeing her lovely face again and taking her in my arms after two long years and all the suffering she had gone through was, of course, overwhelming. The sad news was, however, that both her parents had died; her father from exhaustion in Bergen-Belsen, and her mother only a few days ago in Tröbitz. But her sister Klara who had recovered from typhus only recently, was there to welcome me. When I went to kiss her hello I was outraged to see that, even on her pyjamas, she was still wearing the yellow star! I tore it off immediately and told her in no uncertain words that I did not want to see it on her ever again.

I had brought some English tea, some biscuits and English cigarettes none of which they had seen for many years. There was, of course, a lot to talk about which we did over a nice cup of tea. They told me that most of their relatives fortunately had not only survived the starvation in Bergen-Belsen but also the awful ten-day train journey, when they had been packed into freight carriages, without food or water and had even occasionally been shot at by Allied planes. In the end, most of them had caught typhus and had been taken to the make-shift hospital in Tröbitz.

One of their cousins was upstairs on the second floor also recovering from typhus. The disease had made him so confused that he did not recognise anyone and refused to put on his clothes. I went to see him. Stark naked, he just greeted me with a casual: "Hello Henk!" as if he had seen me only yesterday! These were to be the only sensible words he would speak for some time. Eventually, however, he made a full recovery, body and mind.

The family was actually as comfortable as they could be, in a nice, large, well-appointed house, full of good bedding and the generously filled pantry one would expect from an accomplished German housewife – all of which had been commandeered for them by the Russians. I could not really do anything more to help them, other than go back to Mühlberg and try to find a way to take them safely home as soon as possible. As I had to avoid being seen by the Russians, I stealthily left Tröbitz along some little back streets and bicycled back to the camp.

GOING HOME

Back there I found that most of the Dutch POWs, under the command
of Bob Potter, had been marched off to Leipzig, the first leg of their
trip home. Two clerks, Jan Kok and Hans de Roo, and some nurses
had been left behind to look after those Dutch patients who were still
too ill to be moved. As there was now no Dutch doctor left in the
hospital, the Russian commandant considered the fact that I was a
medical student a good enough reason to make me Director of the
hospital with particular responsibility for the Dutch patients. This
meant, however, that I now had to ask the commandant permission to
leave the hospital grounds, which very much upset my plans to go and
fetch my girlfriend.

Every morning I had to attend the "Soviet", the meeting of all
Heads of Department, where the instructions for the day were given
and only brief remarks could be made. Then breakfast was served,
traditionally a thick pea-soup cooked with pork. To cut the grease, we
were also given a generous tot of vodka. As I still spoke no Russian, a
Yugoslav POW translated for me into French. On the third day I made
him request if, after the Soviet, I could see the Commandant to discuss
a problem. I told the commandant the moving story of how the Nazis
had deported my fiancée from our hometown, that she had been taken
to a concentration camp where she had narrowly escaped death and
had just recently been liberated by the Red Army and that she was now
being cared for in a nearby village. (I was careful not to mention the
name Tröbitz because of the quarantine!) Considering that I had not
seen her for two whole years, could I please go and fetch her? After
looking at me in silence for a moment, he burst out: "Your *fiancée!*, Two
years!, I haven't seen my *wife* in more than *five* years! Dismissed!!"

Two days later I tried again. I told him that I was worried that some
of the Dutch patients might sue me, when back in Holland, for treating
them while still unqualified. But there would not be a problem if I
worked under the supervision of a qualified physician – and I just

ABOVE The open gate at the Mews.

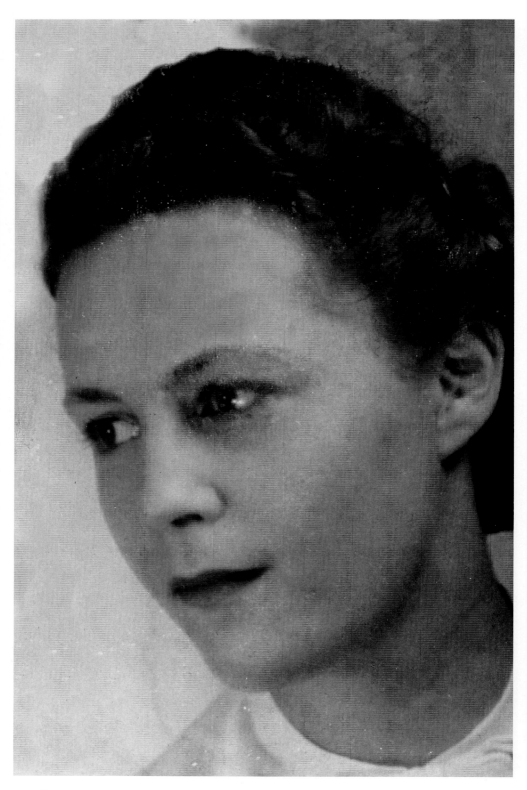

ABOVE Saartje aged 26, circa 1942, a year before being deported.

ABOVE Herman Hammelburg, head nurse, Mühlberg POW camp, 1944. Portrait drawn by Henk Pelser.

ABOVE Prisoners line up facing the wall at Scheveningen Prison.

ABOVE A prisoner in a typical cell at "Oranje Hotel" Scheveningen Prison.

ABOVE The main gate at Stalag IV B, Mühlberg.

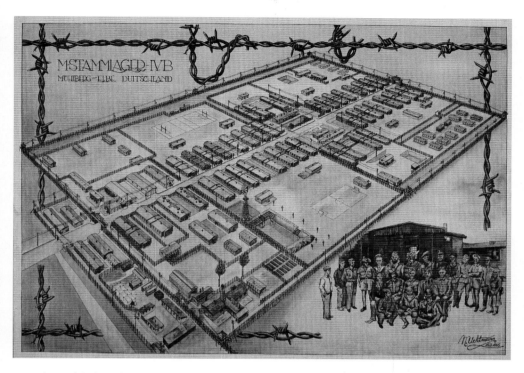

ABOVE An aerial plan of Mühlberg, drawn by fellow POW, N. Uchtmann.

ABOVE Mühlberg camp: taken during the later part of the war. Bob Potter is seated in front row, second from the left, and Henk can be seen looking to the right immediately above the officer fourth from the left.

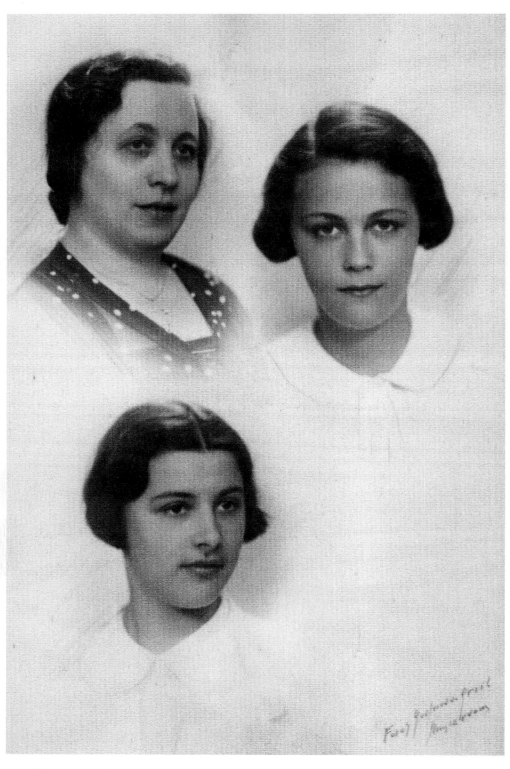

ABOVE The women of Saartje's family before the war: her mother Fijtje Oudkerk, Saartje and her sister Klara. Fijtje died in Tröbitz, days after liberation from Bergen-Belsen. Her husband died in the camp.

ABOVE Reunited. Henk and Saartje's wedding,
August 21st, 1945.

RIGHT Gregory McKay (formerly Speelman),
"the baby in the rucksack", pictured with
Saartje and Henk Pelser in 2003.

ABOVE Saartje and Henk Pelser in 2005. The couple celebrated their Diamond Wedding anniversary.

ABOVE Henk Pelser, 2005.

ABOVE Saartje Pelser, Amsterdam, 2005.

happened to know that there was a Dutch doctor in a nearby village (Jaap Elte of course!). Could I please go and fetch him? The commandant looked at me as if he could not believe his ears! "This is the greatest nonsense I have ever heard!" he barked, "The surgeon who works here is a butcher by trade. He was given six months' surgical training and is now carving up people who would otherwise just damn well perish! There is a goddamn war on, you fool! Dismissed!"

I had now figured out that the commandant knew nothing about medicine but was simply a good administrator put in this job to make things run smoothly. So, to have it my way, I should offer him a problem that, although it made no medical sense, might seriously upset the smooth running of the hospital if he did not deal with it. I gave it four days before I dared make my next move. Not unnaturally, he was very suspicious when I asked to talk to him again, but when I told him I had a major problem with the laboratory, he appeared at least willing to listen. I explained that, as the laboratory results were written in Russian, I was unable to read them, which made it difficult for me to do my job. But that I could get a qualified Dutch laboratory technician (Saartje!) who just happened to live nearby, so if he would allow me to go and fetch her, she could do the laboratory work for me and at the same time relieve the greatly overworked Russian technicians. This at last seemed to strike a chord and after thinking it over for a minute, he not only agreed but also ordered me a horse-drawn cart and coachman.

And thus it was, that on the 31st of May, 1945, Saartje's 29th birthday, I was at last happily on my way to fetch her and her sister from Tröbitz, riding precariously on the box of some German farmer's cart, next to an elderly Moscovite coachman with a black drooping moustache. He was wrapped in a filthy old cloak and the wreaths of smoke belching forth from his *mahorka*, the foul smelling home-grown tobacco of the Russian farmers, which was always rolled in scraps of newspaper and invariably drew tears from the eyes of anybody getting too close.

To avoid the Russian guards in Tröbitz, I made him take the back-road I had used the other day and thus we arrived safely at the house where Saartje's family lived.

As she was still too weak to walk, I had to carry Saartje downstairs, which was no effort at all in her condition. In spite of my assurances that there was plenty to eat in Mühlberg, Klara insisted on bringing with her what seemed to be the better part of the contents of the well-stocked pantry. In my efforts to dissuade her, I even had to resort to the use of foul language and when, eventually, she was left tearfully clutching a single jar of pea soup, she presented such a sorry sight that I relented.

Jaap Elte was enviously watching the preparations for his nieces' departure from this place where he was living in constant dread of catching typhus. When I asked him if he would like to join us, he jumped at the suggestion and rushed to pack the few things he wanted to take.

And so, on a beautiful summer day, the four of us were driven through the countryside, as though we did not have a care in the world, chatting in pidgin German with our colourful coachman, who wanted to know where we came from. Jaap Elte told him: "From Amsterdam, in the West somewhere, a long, long way away from here". The coachman had never heard of it. He only knew Rotterdam which had been savagely bombed by the Nazis. But even that was not half as far away from here as Moscow, he said. We looked at each other in disbelief, but later found that he had been quite right, of course!

When we arrived at the Mühlberg hospital, the commandant could hardly fail to notice that the qualified laboratory technician I had promised him had to be carried inside, obviously too weak to stand on her feet. He must have realised that he had been had, but graciously never said a word about it.

To welcome my girlfriend and her sister, Jan Kok and Hans de Roo had baked them a delicious cake, which however, was so rich that they could eat only a few crumbs. They had been deprived of such delicacies for so long that their digestive system simply could not cope!

I put them immediately on a strict diet of frequent small meals, consisting mainly of carbohydrates and protein, a little dairy fat, and massive doses of vitamins. Under this regime they rapidly gained strength. Every day the Russians provided us with a large joint of beef, about a pound per person. Jaap Elte, an accomplished pathologist, would sit for hours, like a proper kosher butcher doing his porshing, or dissecting away all vessels and sinewy parts. We fried the meat in lots of butter which, most decadently, was then fed to the dog! This was also the way most of the German bread went, as we were given so much that we could not possibly eat it all. When even the dog had had enough, we used the leftover stale bread for fuel in the cooking stove rather than give it to the starving Germans who came begging for it. We knew, of course, that the bounty that the Russians were lavishing on us came from the ransacked local population. At the time we all thought that it was only right that they should know what it was like to go hungry while those in power were feasting in front of them!

The Russians also supplied the hospital with abundant food, but apparently they had not the slightest notion of dietary treatment. Each patient, whatever his medical condition, was given his daily ration of German bread, sugar, and a rather generous measure of vodka. One day I was summoned by the Commandant of the hospital who reprimanded me severely for depriving some of my patients of the German bread and the sugar to which they were entitled. My defence, that they were suffering from severe diarrhoea and needed a sugar-free diet and rusks instead of rye bread, made not the slightest impression. He accused me of robbing "members of the proletariat under his protection" of their rightful share, and for this he could have me shot! I protested that I was just providing standard medical care to MY patients, but he retorted that this was utter nonsense and had to stop immediately or else!

So I had no choice but to explain to the patients in question why, in their own interest, they should not eat the bread and the sugar they were given by the Russians. Unfortunately many of them were just too ravenous to take my advice and some of them actually ate themselves to death!

Meanwhile, Saartje who, much to her disgust, had been spoon-fed a bowl of porridge and cream every morning, had sufficiently recovered to be able to stand on her feet and, after about a week, she even felt strong enough to do a little work in the laboratory, just to show willing.

Then, out of the blue, some ambulances arrived from the West. As we just happened to be the nearest hospital in the Soviet zone, they were bringing us some badly emaciated and diseased Russians who had been liberated from Nazi concentration camps. The ambulance drivers were French women whose tidy uniforms and immaculate make-up gave a rude shock to Saartje and Klara who had quite forgotten what a woman was supposed to look like! For my part, I was far more interested to see if I could not persuade these charming ladies to take my patients and my party with them on their return trip. After some deliberation they agreed, on condition that I would take full responsibility for the patients' medical care and their onward transportation from Leipzig, which was as far as they were going. Although I did not have even the faintest idea how I was going to accomplish all this, I readily agreed. Perhaps most delighted of all at our sudden departure was the Russian Commandant, who made no secret of his relief to be rid of thirty Dutch patients of very uncertain health and their most troublesome doctor.

So we all hurriedly packed into the ambulances and, after a comfortable drive through the American zone, safely arrived at a make-shift temporary hospital which had been set up in a Leipzig school.

Here, for the first time in my life I saw patients, mainly American servicemen, who had, literally been blinded from drinking copious quantities of local schnapps which, due to the shortages, had been adulterated with methanol.

It soon became clear that the civil administration and organisation in Leipzig had, most un-German like, completely broken down. Apparently the recent announcement that the city was soon to be handed over to the Russians had caused so much panic that even the hospital management was only interested in looking for ways to get to the West. So, the day after we arrived, Jaap Elte and I were invited to the office of the hospital director who gravely received us as *hochverehrten Kollegen* (distinguished colleagues) but was obviously also in the grip of the general Russo-phobia. It did not take him long to pop the question if we could please take his wife and two daughters with us to the West to save them from a fate worse than death. Jaap and I looked at each other and were just about to agree, when the German, in an effort to add some weight to his request, added pompously: *"Schliesslich sind wir doch ein Kulturvolk, oder?"* (we are, after all, civilised people, aren't we?) Jaap Elte turned puce, banged his fist on the table, and exploded: *"SIE ein KULTURVOLK?! Ich sage Ihnen dass in Deutschland mit Goethe der LETZTE Kulturmensch ist gestorben!"* (YOU!, CIVILISED?! Let me tell you that the last civilised German died with GOETHE!).

After this, it was unnecessary to continue the conversation and we left him to his thoughts.

Needless to say, this incident did nothing to improve the zeal of the hospital staff to look after our patients and it made us even more determined to get out of the place as soon as possible.

Jan Kok and Hans de Roo took up position at the railway station watching for any train going west. Only two days later Hans de Roo came running to tell me that a hospital train was due carrying Russian patients liberated from concentration camps who were to continue home by truck. I rushed to the station where the empty train was still standing and found the commanding officer, Matron Brown, an American army nurse. I told her, with an apparently convincing air of authority, that I was requisitioning her train for the transport of some thirty Dutch patients from Bergen-Belsen whom I urgently needed to get back home, together with my nursing staff. It obviously never occurred to her that someone without any official status would have the barefaced gall to pull such a stunt. All she did, was object that there were no facilities on the train to prepare cooked meals for so many patients, but when I laughed and said that they had been through worse and would happily settle for emergency rations during the trip, she agreed to take us. Back at the hospital, our news was greeted with great enthusiasm and everybody started to get ready to leave. Now experienced, we quickly commandeered some trucks and took our little flock to the waiting train. And soon we were finally on the last leg of our journey home!

From the unaccustomed luxury of our very comfortable stretchers we surveyed, with a sensation of grim satisfaction, the massive destruction which the Allied bombing had wrought on the German cities we passed. Watching German women and children rummaging through the rubble for something to eat filled us then with a wonderful sense of just retribution!

We travelled for a good three days till, on June 18th, 1945, we finally arrived at the railway station in Eindhoven.

My first job was to go and hand over responsibility for my patients to the proper authorities. When I came back I found, to my fury, that Saartje had been arrested! Some bloody fool had thought her an impostor because she did not look Jewish and seemed too well fed to have been in a concentration camp! Fuming with rage I rushed to yell at the authorities but, as none of us had identity papers, it got me absolutely nowhere. Fortunately, I suddenly found a friend from university. He was there checking for tuberculosis amongst the repatriates from the German concentration camps and was soon able to clear up this preposterous situation. The local authorities had apparently, in spite of five years' Nazi occupation, not lost any of their pre-war addiction to bureaucracy.

What a welcome!

My friend managed to organise a van to take us to Amsterdam. We said good-bye to Jan Kok and Hans de Roo, who were going home to The Hague, and were soon travelling the last hundred miles to Amsterdam where, after five long and very eventful years, we could finally start thinking about building a new life.

EPILOGUE

The above events occurred more than half a century ago and have never been fully recorded in official documents. This is probably also why there are a number of omissions in the magnum opus of the historian Dr. L. de Jong, *Het Koninkrijk der Nederlanden in de Tweede Wereldoorlog* (The Kingdom of The Netherlands in the Second World War) which is the official record of that period published by the NIOD (National Institute for War Documentation).

Dr. de Jong based himself largely on written records. These could be anything from private letters to documents of the German police and administration. In doing so he made no allowance for the fact that members of the Resistance, when caught, not only would be likely to be less than truthful to their interrogators but also had proven ways of giving disinformation that would not be found out. Volume 6, part 1, and volume 7, part 2, consequently supply an incomplete record of the way in which the so-called "Swiss route B", the connection between the Resistance and the Dutch Government-in-exile, was established. Nor is it mentioned that our route to Switzerland continued to be used for the transport of people and information until at least April 1944, when Jet Rosenburg was arrested and tried as a member of "Fiat Libertas", the famous group that organised the escape of Allied pilots who had been shot down over enemy territory.

The fact that, after we had been arrested in April 1943, we managed to keep our trip to Switzerland from our Nazi interrogators, undoubtedly saved our lives but, at the same time, it meant that the information recorded in the official German documents did not reflect the truth.

There is little contest when one is presented with the choice between survival and historical accuracy. My choice at least has given me the chance to correct the historian's history.

HISTORICAL CONTEXT

1938

09.11   "Kristallnacht"

1939

1938/1939   my trips to Germany
28.08   general mobilisation in the Netherlands
03.09   German invasion of Poland; start of the
               Second World War

1940

10.05   German invasion of The Netherlands
14.05   bombardment of Rotterdam
18.05   appointment of Seyss-Inquart
27.05-04.06   evacuation of Dunkirk
29.06   birthday of Prince Bernhard: "carnation day"
25.07   first publication of the "newsletter of Pieter 't Hoen"
September   move into "het Suyckerhofje"
October   civil servants are required to sign declaration of Aryan
               parentage
26.11   Professor Cleveringa holds his speech at Leiden
               University

1941

February   introduction to Lex Althof; first contact with *Het
               Parool*
25.02   the February strike
22.06   German invasion of Russia
07.12   Japanese attack on Pearl Harbour

1942

January	open letter to the Rector Magnificus
18.01	Frans Goedhart is arrested
April	wearing the yellow star becomes compulsory
21.06	fall of Tobruk
July	first deportations from the Netherlands
19.08	British raid on Dieppe
	I cross the Belgian border for the first time
September	Smedts and I travel via Brussels to Besançon
October	my journey Brussels-Besançon-Lyon-Annemasse-Geneva-Chateauneuf-les-Bains-Lyon-Nancy-Brussels (arrival 04.11.42)
27.10	Van Norden is arrested
28.10	Jan Meijer and Jaap Nunes Vaz are arrested
04.11	Smedts is arrested
08.11	allied invasion of northern Africa
11.11	Hitler occupies Vichy-France
27.11	Ward and Juta Messer are arrested
02.12	journey with Ekker: Brussels-Bouillon-Sedan-Belfort
05.12	Belfort-Paris
08.12	back in Amsterdam

1943

06.01	Ekker and I depart for Switzerland
09.01	arrival in Belfort
14.01	arrival in Bern
16.01	Fremdenstube zur Heimat
20.01	to Cossonay
26.01	publication report of Casablanca conference
31.01	capitulation German VI army at Stalingrad
19.02	we return via Porrentruy-Sedan-Brussels
21.02	arrival in Amsterdam

27.03	raid on Amsterdam municipal archives
02.04	Ekker is arrested
03.04	I am arrested
13.05	German capitulation in North Africa

1944

14.03	in court before the Obergericht
15.03	on PoW transport to Mühlberg
06.06	D-Day
25.07	Mussolini deposed
08.09	capitulation of Italy
17.09	Operation "Market Garden"; beginning of the battle of Arnhem
December	Ardennes offensive
24.12	American POW's arrive in Mühlberg

1945

07.03	American troops cross the Rhine
22.04	German guards abandon the Mühlberg camp
30.04	Hitler's suicide
05.05	the Germans capitulate in the Netherlands
17.05	to Tröbitz
31.05	I collect Saartje, Klara and Jaap Elte
12.06	to Leipzig
18.06	arrival in Eindhoven and Amsterdam

BIOGRAPHICAL DETAILS

We have tried to collect short biographical details of some of the people who are mentioned in this book, mainly to inform the reader what happened to them after the period covered by these memoirs. Sadly, there are several individuals whom we would have liked to include but on whom we could not discover any meaningful information.

Althoff, A.A.F. (Lex) -

Born in Haarlem in 1905. In 1940 he was editor in charge of the nightshift at the newspaper *Het Volk*. He also published two novels. He was arrested on May 22nd, 1942, and executed in Utrecht on July 20th, 1943.

Arondeus, Willem J.C. -

Born in Naarden in August 1894. Together with the artist Gerrit van der Veen, he carried out the raid on the Amsterdam municipal register on March 27th, 1943. He was arrested on April 1st, 1943, and executed on July 1st of that year.

von Balluseck, D.J. -

Born March 8th, 1895 in Utrecht. On July 7th, 1941 he was arrested and, because of his incessant criticism of the nazi occupation, was dismissed from his position as chief editor of the quality newspaper *Algemeen Handelsblad*. After a month he was released, but in December 1941 he was again detained and not released till September 1944. After the war he returned to his position at the *Algemeen Handelsblad* until his appointment, on February 1st 1950, as permanent representative of the Netherlands at the United Nations. He was subsequently appointed as representative at the Security Council. From August 1955 until November 1957 he was Dutch ambassador in Moscow and thereafter, until his retirement, ambassador in Canada. He died on March 3rd, 1985, in The Hague.

de Beaufort, B.Ph., Jhr. -

Born August 17th, 1919 in Arnhem. He studied at the agricultural university at Wageningen. On November 4th, 1942, he was arrested in Brussels, together with Mathieu Smedts and Anja Horowitz. On July 1st, 1943, he managed to escape from the sick bay of Scheveningen prison. In September 1944 he joined a sabotage group of the *Binnenlandse Strijdkrachten* (the underground "army" under the supreme command of Prince Bernhard which was to prepare the ground for liberation). On February 16th, 1945, he was recognised by a Nazi policeman in Amsterdam and, in his attempt to escape, fell to his death from a window.

van Beverwijk, Lien, -

Born September19th, 1914. In 1941 she was working as resident at the department of psychiatry and neurology of one of the teaching hospitals in Amsterdam, the Wilhelmina Gasthuis. She was arrested in 1942, but released again fairly quickly as her professor declared that it was impossible for her to be involved in illegal activities, as she was busy in the hospital day and night. After the war she worked at the Institute for Psycho-Analysis where she was involved in the post-graduate training of psychiatrists. In the 1970's she was very involved in the establishment of the Institute of Medical Psychology. She died February 27th, 1996 in Amsterdam.

Cleveringa, R.P., -

Born in 1894 in Appingedam. In 1927 he was appointed Professor of Law at Leiden university. On November 26th, 1940, he held his protest lecture at Leiden and was arrested two days later. In March 1941 he was dismissed from his post by the occupation administration. In the summer of 1941 he was released and went to live in De Steeg, in the province of Gelderland. In January 1944 he was detained again and held in the internment camp at Vught until the middle of that year.

After the war he headed the Cleveringa Commission charged with the investigation of complaints against the wartime behaviour of official Dutch representatives in France, Spain, Switzerland and Portugal. In 1958 he was made a member of the *Raad van State*, the highest governmental advisory body in the Netherlands. He published several standard textbooks on maritime and civil law. He died December 15th, 1980.

Dutilh, C.C. (Kees) -

Born March 5th, 1915. He was the leader of the spy-group codenamed "Kees". On March 10th, 1943, he was arrested as one of the victims of the *Englandspiel* and was executed on February 24th, 1944.

Ekker, A., (Dries) -

Born October 9th, 1917 in Amsterdam. After he was released from nazi imprisonment in July 1944 he headed the Utrecht branch of the illegal *Het Parool*. On the very day that Utrecht was liberated he brought out the newspaper under the name *Nieuw Utrechts Dagblad*. Later he was parliamentary editor of *Het Parool* and editor-in-chief of a conglomerate of regional daily newspapers based in The Hague. In 1968 he was appointed Cultural- and Press Attaché at the Dutch embassy in Mexico and later occupied the same position at the Washington embassy. He died on June 12th, 1990, in Naarden.

Elte, J., -

Born May 3rd, 1895 in Den Helder. He was a physician and later became medical director of the *Binnengasthuis*, one of the Amsterdam teaching hospitals. He died September 25th, 1984, in Amsterdam.

Frenkel, M., -

Born June 1st, 1919 in Goes. He returned from Switzerland in the summer of 1945 and started his training as a physician with Dr. J.J.

Groen in Amsterdam. In 1956 he was appointed deputy director of the *Wilhelmina Gasthuis* in Amsterdam. In 1960 he was appointed head of the department of internal medicine at the hospital for oncology, *Anthonie van Leeuwenhoekhuis* in Amsterdam. In 1967 he was appointed professor of internal medicine at Erasmus University in Rotterdam.

Frenkel, S., -

Born December 10th, 1920 in Goes. He finished his medical studies in Lausanne and specialised in microbiology. He later occupied a staff position at the government veterinary institute in Lelystad where he conducted research in the areas of microbiology and virology.

Goedhart, F.J. (Frans) -
alias Pieter 't Hoen.

Born January 25th, 1904 in Amsterdam. In December 1942 he was sentenced to death by the *Fieldgericht* in Utrecht. On 2nd August 1943 he escaped from the police station at Vught. After the war he wrote a column for Het Parool under his alias. He was chairman of the Foundation *Het Parool* until 1956. In the autumn of 1945 he became a member of the emergency parliament. He remained a member of the second chamber of parliament until 1972. He died March 3rd, 1990.

de Groot, C.H., (Cees) -

Born 1913 in The Hague. He was arrested in Amsterdam at the beginning of March 1945 and, together with dozens of others, executed on March 9th near Rozenoord on the river Amstel as a reprisal for the attack on Rauter at Woeste Hoeve.

Hammelburg, H.I. (Herman) -

On June 14th, 1945, he and the rest of the remaining nursing staff were transported to Leipzig airport by jeep and then flown to Eindhoven by DC3. Upon his arrival all his personal possessions had vanished. He later emigrated to Israel where he was on the board of directors of a general hospital and was head of its outpatients department.

van Heuven Goedhart, G.J., (Ger) -

Born March 19th, 1901 in Bussum. On April 25th, 1944, he left via the underground route through Spain to arrive in London on June 17th. On July 12th he was appointed Minister of Justice of the Dutch government-in-exile. On August 27th, 1945 he became Editor-in-Chief of *Het Parool*. Later he was a member of the upper house of parliament and, from January 1st, 1951, he was High Commissioner for Refugees at the United Nations in Geneva where he died suddenly in 1956.

Kann, Maurits -

Born in 1894 in The Hague. He was arrested in the spring of 1941 and executed at the end of March 1942 in Sachsenhausen.

Laqueur, Renata, -

Born November 3rd, 1919. On July 4th, 1945, she left Zeithain and, after many detours, arrived in Maastricht on July 22nd, 1945. She published her *Diary from Bergen-Belsen*. Later she moved to the United States where she studied comparative linguistics and wrote her doctorate thesis on diaries written in concentration camps.

Maillette de Buy Wenniger, H.E. (Herman), -

Born September 1st, 1909. In 1944 he was appointed personnel manager at a chemical company in Delft. Later he was head of public relations at Gist Brocades. He retired to his wonderful Château de St. Martin de las Oumettes in southern France where he lived till shortly before his death in Amsterdam in 1986.

Meijer, Jan, -

Born March 30th, 1914 in Arnhem. After the war he and Wim van Norden were both director at *Het Parool*. He was a Board Member of the Foundation *Het Parool* until his statutory retirement on his 70th birthday. From the end of 1948 he worked at the department of international organisations at the Ministry of Foreign Affairs, from where he eventually retired as director-general. He died on March 2nd, 1997.

Meijers, E.M. -

Born January 10th, 1880 in Den Helder. He obtained his doctorate "cum laude" in Amsterdam in 1903 and was appointed Professor of Law at the university of Leiden in 1910. In November 1940 he was dismissed by the Nazi occupier and later sent to Theresienstadt where he remained in captivity for three years. He returned to Leiden on June 25th, 1945. In 1947 he was commissioned to write a new civil code of law, of which he finished the first half just before his death on June 25th, 1954.

Messer, E. (Ward) -

Born July 9th, 1917 in Amsterdam. After the liberation he and Ekker together ran the Utrecht office of *Het Parool*. Later he was managing editor at *Het Vrije Volk* where he was appointed editor-in-chief on April 1st, 1968. From 1970 until his retirement in 1977 he was managing director of Het Vrije Volk in Rotterdam. He died on November 14th, 2001.

Messer-Grünbaum, A.J., (Juta) -

Born April 24th, 1917. After her release from the Amstelveenseweg jail at the beginning of June 1943, she spent the rest of the war in Amsterdam and Doornspijk. Because she was married to a Gentile she was more or less safe from deportation. After Toontje she had two more children. She died August 6th, 1992.

Mussert, A.A., -

On May 7th, 1945 he was executed on the Waalsdorper Vlakte, in the dunes near The Hague. His body was buried in a secret place.

Noach, S., (Sally) -

Born December 29th, 1909 in Zutphen. To escape the *razzias* in Lyon he left for London via de Spanish route at the end of 1942. Although he was received by Queen Wilhelmina, the Dutch authorities did not give him much recognition for the work that he had done in France. On December 24th, 1969 Queen Juliana invested him with the Order of the House Order of Orange which is a personal Royal prerogative. After the war he returned to his business trading oriental rugs. He died on March 31st, 1980 in Amsterdam.

van Norden, Wim -

Born June 13th, 1917 in Bussum. After the war he was secretary and member of the Board of *Stichting Het Parool* and managing director of the newspaper *Het Parool*. From 1968 to 1979 he was chairman of the board at Perscombinatie and later became a member of the supervisory board. He was also chairman of the Dutch press association, *Nederlandse Dagblad Pers*. He is honorary chairman of the Foundation *Het Parool*.

Nunes Vaz, Jaap -

Born in 1907. He was an editor at ANP, the Dutch press service, until he was dismissed in 1940 for being a Jew. On October 25th, 1942 he was arrested at his *onderduik* address, his safe house, at the home of Pierre Helderman in Wageningen en subsequently deported to Sobibor where he died.

Nyst, Margot -

Born 1911. She survived the war and is still living in Brussels.

van Oss, Carel Jan, -

Born September 7th, 1923 in Amsterdam. He was arrested in November 1942 and was held captive in the "Orange Hotel", the jail in Scheveningen for a period of three months. He remained very active as a forger of documents right up to the end of the war. After the liberation he was appointed intelligence officer by the RAF to check the reliability of new Dutch military recruits who were to be trained in Britain. He studied physical biochemistry and did his doctorate in Paris in 1955. In 1967 he was appointed professor of microbiology at the medical faculty of the State University of New York at Buffalo, where he is now also adjunct-professor in the fields of chemical technology and geology.

Oudkerk, Sarah (Saartje) -

Born May 31st, 1916 in Amsterdam. She trained to be a pharmacist assistant and medical laboratory analyst. She was head of the laboratory of the Dutch-Israelitic Hospital in Amsterdam until she was deported in September 1943. On August 21st, 1945 she married Henk Pelser.

Oudkerk, Klara -

Born 13th May 1911 in Amsterdam. After the war she again took up her profession of social worker. She studied casework in Cleveland, Ohio from 1950 to 1952. Later she worked at the Berg Foundation in Laren and thereafter, until her retirement, at Le Ezrath Hajeled in Amsterdam.

Pelser, Henk -

Born July 17th, 1916 in Bandung, Dutch East Indies. He came to Amsterdam in 1933 to finish his schooling and then read medicine at the University of Amsterdam. He became a physician and gained a Ph.D. in internal medicine in 1954. He practised at the university hospital in Amsterdam, known as the *Wilhelmina Gasthuis,* where he worked in the areas of psychosomatic medicine and endocrinology. He continued his involvement with *Het Parool* as a member of the Board of the foundation that owns the newspaper. He is medical advisor and Honorary Member of the Foundation 1940–1945 which provides support to members of the resistance and victims of persecution and war. His work for the Foundation gave him valuable insight into the long term psychological and physical consequences of persecution and resistance work. In 1992 he was invited to Moscow to advise on the assistance to be given to victims of the gulags. On April 16th, 1996 the Israeli Ambassador to the Netherlands, on behalf of Yad Vashem, the Israeli Holocaust memorial authority, invested Henk Pelser as Righteous Amongst the Nations in recognition of his efforts to save Jewish lives during the Second World War. Henk Pelser and his wife Saartje have two daughters and five grandchildren. They live in Amsterdam.

van Poppel, Jozef -
alias Meesters

He was originally from the southern province of Brabant and had joined the Dutch Nazi party early on. Even before the war he already worked for the German *Abwehr* in Amsterdam, where he had many contacts in the criminal world. After the invasion he moved to Belgium with instructions to recruit agents for the *Abwehr* who could be infiltrated into Britain. After the war he was brought to justice, declared insane and consigned to an institution.

van der Putten, D. -

Born December 11th, 1906. After the war he was transferred to Paris where he was chief executive of Philips. Later he became a member of the board of directors at Philips' head office in Eindhoven. He retired to the South of France where he died in the spring of 1998.

Roosenburg, H. (Jet) -

Born May 26th, 1916. In April 1944 she was arrested and, at her July trial, sentenced to death for her work with Fiat Libertas, the organisation that helped Allied pilots. In the confusion of the allied invasion the sentence was not carried out and she was sent to prison in Germany. On May 7th, 1945, she was liberated by the Russians in Waldheim, Saxony. She eventually moved to the United States where she had a job as correspondent with *Time/Life Magazine*. She described her journey back home in her book *The Walls Came Tumbling Down*. She moved to the United States where she had a job as correspondent with *Time/Life Magazine*. In 1966 she moved to her house in the South of France where she died in 1972.

Seyss-Inquart, A., -

Born July 22nd, 1892, in Stannern, Austria. He was taken prisoner on May 7th, 1945, when he was returning from a meeting with Admiral Dönitz in a German motor-torpedoboat that was, quite by coincidence, challenged by a Canadian patrol vessel. On October 1st, 1946, he was sentenced to death at the Nurenberg trials and executed by hanging on October 16th, 1946.

Sindram, Emil, -

Born July 5th, 1915. From 1949 - 1964 he worked at the Institute for Public Health in the Dutch Antilles, first as chemist and later as managing director. He later moved back to Arnhem where he was head of the laboratory of the municipal hospital until his retirement. He has since died.

Smedts, P.M. (Mathieu) -
alias Mat van den Berg

Born May 26th, 1913 in Grashoek, Limburg. After he was sentenced to death on November 17th, 1943, the Nazis made him disappear into *Nacht und Nebel*. He was liberated by the Russians on April 27th, 1945 from the prison-camp at Wolfenbüttel. After the war he first worked for the daily *de Volkskrant* and then, from 1955 to 1969, he was editor-in-chief of the weekly *Vrij Nederland*. He published extensively about his experiences during the war and also about his travels abroad. He died August 11th, 1996 in Amsterdam.

Speelman, W., -

Born May 8th, 1911. After their arrival in Switzerland the Speelmans were first in two refugee camps and then moved to *residence forcée*. Speelman joined the Dutch Army and went with them from Switzerland to Holland. On May 10th, 1945 he was in Amsterdam. His wife and child joined him several months later. In 1951 they emigrated to Canada where he taught physics and chemistry at the university of Toronto. In 1954 they moved to California where he joined the board of a chemical company. After his retirement in 1973 he has been doing research in the field of theoretical physics. His eldest son (born 1942) is an economist and lives in Los Angeles.

van Stokkum, D.J. (Dick) -

Born February 18th, 1915. He was arrested on April 2nd, 1943. He was released without trial in 1944 for lack of evidence. He became head of transport at *Het Parool*, later studied dentistry and set up his practice in Amsterdam in 1953. He died November 9th, 1976.

Visser 't Hooft, W.A., -

Born September 20th, 1900 in Haarlem. In 1939 he was appointed secretary-general of the embryonic World Council of Churches in

Geneva. He was confirmed in this position in 1948 and remained there until his retirement in 1966. He remained an adviser and honorary chairman of the organisation until he died in Geneva on July 4th, 1985.

Warendorf, J.C.S., -

Born April 15th, 1902 in Amsterdam. After the war he was legal adviser to Unesco in Paris and lived in Versailles during that time. In 1948 he moved back to Amsterdam where he set up his own law practice specialising in Anglo-American law. From the outset he was a Board Member of Foundation *Het Parool* until he reached the statutory retirement age in 1972. He was a sworn translator and chairman of the Netherlands Association of Translators. It was largely due to his efforts that the University of Amsterdam established an institute to further the training of translators and interpreters. He died on October 15th, 1987 in Amersfoort.

NOTES

Note 1 *page 31 – passeur –* these were men and women who, for payment, would take people across borders via routes that avoided check-points and border controls. *Passeurs* became more and more expensive, but they were generally reliable.

Note 2 *page 62 – Outsiplou –* this was the code name of a heroic Belgian freedom fighter who fought the Germans during the first world war.

Note 3 *page 64 – Jonkheer* is a very old Dutch title, roughly the equivalent of Baronet.

Note 4 *page 103 –* The Municipal Registration Office contains files of all inhabitants of a municipality, showing names, addresses, age, religion and other personal details. Access to these files obviously made it very easy to locate the Jewish population. On March 27th, 1943 a resistance group led by Gerrit van der Veen and Willem Arondeus torched the Amsterdam office. Shortly afterwards they were betrayed and the entire group was executed on July 1st, 1943.

BIBLIOGRAPHY

K.W.L. Bezemer, *"Geschiedenis van de Nederlandse Koopvaardij in de Tweede Wereldoorlog"* – Elsevier Boeken B.V., 1986

H. van den Heuvel/G. Mulder, *"Het Vrije Woord"* – SDU 1990

Dr. L. de Jong, *"Het Koninkrijk der Nederlanden in de Tweede Wereldoorlog"*

Dr. L. de Jong, *"De Bezetting"*, Querido 1964

A.F. Manning/H. Balthazar/Joh. de Vries (red.), *"Algemene Geschiedenis der Nederlanden"* – deel 15 – Fibula-Van Dishoeck, 1982

H.M. van Randwijk, *"In de Schaduw van Gisteren"* – Bert Bakker et al, 4e druk 1968

Mathieu Smedts, *"Den Vaderland Getrouwe"* – Arbeiderspers 1962

Mathieu Smedts, *"Waarheid en Leugen in het verzet"* – Corrie Zelen, 1e druk 1978

Gerlof Verwey, *"Geschiedenis van Nederland"*, Elsevier 1987

Evert Werkman, *"Ik néém het niet"*, A.W. Sijthoff 1965